Abiding
in
Christ

Books by Paul J. Bucknell

Allowing the Bible to speak to our lives today!

* Overcoming Anxiety: Finding Peace, Discovering God
* Reaching Beyond Mediocrity: Faith's Triumph Over Temptation
* The Life Core: Discovering the Heart of Great Training
* Life in the Spirit! Experiencing the Fullness of Christ
* The Making of A Godly Leader: Isaiah 53, The Fourth Servant Song
* The Godly Man: When God Touches a Man's Life
* Redemption Through the Scriptures/ Study Guide
* Godly Beginnings for the Family
* Principles and Practices of Biblical Parenting
* Building a Great Marriage
* A Biblical Perspective on Social Justice: A Christian View of Reparation
* The Lord Your Healer: Discover Him and Find…
* Christian Premarital Counseling Manual for Counselors
* Relational Discipleship: Cross Training
* A Spiritual Map for Unity
* Quality Times With God: Renew Your Life Through Daily Devotions
* Running the Race: Overcoming Lusts
* The Bible Teaching Commentary on Genesis
* The Bible Teaching Commentary on Romans
* Book of Romans: Bible Study Questions
* Book of Ephesians: Bible Studies
* Abiding in Christ: Walking with Jesus
* Inductive Bible Studies in Titus
* Life Transformation: A Monthly … on Romans 12:9-21
* 1 Peter Bible Study Questions: Living in a Fallen World
* Satan's Four Stations: The Destroyer is Destroyed
* 3 X E Discipleship (Discipler and Disciple)
* Take Your Next Step into Ministry
* Training Leaders for Ministry
* Study Guide for Jonah: Understanding God's Heart

Check out our Discipleship Digital Libraries at
www.foundationsforfreedom.net || www.bflbible.org

Abiding in Christ:

Walking with Jesus

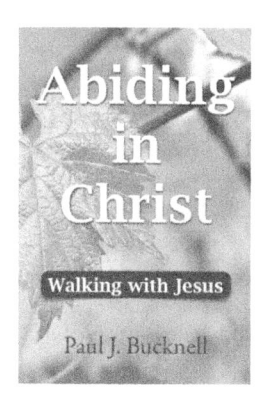

by
Paul J. Bucknell

Book Information

Abiding in Christ: Walking with Jesus

Copyright © 2002, 2016, 2023 by Paul J. Bucknell

    ISBN-13: 978-1-61993-072-8 (Paperback)

    Also in digital

    ISBN-13: 978-1-61993-071-1

www.bffbible.org

www.foundationsforfreedom.net

The NASB is used unless otherwise stated.

New American Standard Bible ©1960, 1995 used by permission, Lockman Foundation www.lockman.org.

Paul J. Bucknell, USA

All rights reserved. Limited production is acceptable without prior permission for home and educational use. For extensive reproduction or other questions, feel free to contact the author at pb@bffbible.org .

Tribute

Love from Heaven

overflows into our lives,

amazed and delighted, we praise our Lord.

In Christ, we bear long-lasting fruit;

His love forever flows from our lives

into the world,

bearing forth His glory.

For Christ, we bear long-lasting fruit

Table of Contents

Book Information	4
Tribute	5
Table of Contents	7
Preface	9
Introduction	15
Impossible Love Mark 8:1-9	19
Genuine Friendship John 15:15-16	25
A Vial of Love Mark 14:1-9	29
Following is Not Easy Mark 10:46-52	35
Listening Carefully Mark 7:17-18	41
A Faith that Counts Mark 11:20-24	47
Staying Focused on God's Will Matthew 15:21-28	51
Discover Your True Treasure Mark 10:21-27	59
Worth It All! Mark 10:28-31	67

Capsizing Religion Mark 3:1-6	73
The Family of Jesus Mark 3:31-35	79
Growing Confidence in Jesus Mark 7:31-37	85
A Word on Christian Suffering John 15:1-2	91
Genuine Worship Mark 12:28-34	99
Dreams to Dust Mark 13:1-3	103
A Faith of Action Mark 11:27-33	107
The Felling of Fame Mark 2:1-2	113
A Perspective on Worry Luke 12:25-26	119
Overcoming the Fear of Man Mark 11:27-33	125
Appendix 1: More on Paul J. Bucknell	131
Appendix 2: Your Personal Notes	133
Appendix 3: About This Book	135

Preface

I did not plan this book! The Lord caught me off-guard, breaking into my daily routine to draw me closer to Himself.

Many years ago, the Lord worked in a specific season to teach me more about meditation in His Word. He knew about my interest in growing as a Christian. However, He wasn't impressed with my past decades of missionary and pastoral work. The Lord wanted to shape my heart further. He initially grabbed my attention by speaking to me through Psalm 1 and Joshua 1 about the need for daily meditation.

> This book of the law shall not depart from your mouth, **but you shall meditate on it** day and night, so that you may be careful to do according to all that is written in it; for then you will make your way prosperous, and then you will have success. (Josh 1:8 NASB used unless noted)

God designed meditation as a way for His people to grow and succeed. My excuses about not having enough time for meditation did not go far. Though I had a hectic schedule and got up early every morning to meet Him, my Heavenly Father sought more time with me. He made that very clear.

I struggled with Him for a while. Eventually, I gave up listening to an afternoon radio talk show so that I could listen to Him speak to me through His Word. The meditation time was not necessarily going to take much time each day, but time was already hard to come by for me as a father of seven and founder of a new ministry. Regardless, I made plans to meet with Him during the afternoon. I could never have imagined what was in store. As I think about it now, I am still astonished and profoundly moved when I think about how the Lord met me during those times.

Above all, I desired to hear from the Lord during those short meditation times, and He certainly delivered. I was utterly changed by my intimate time with Him. The time I spent rarely exceeded thirty minutes, but what He taught me greatly impacted my life. I immediately started to spend more time writing down my thoughts and experiences. The truths were so evident, piercing, and heartbreaking that I felt the need to prepare myself before meeting Him again.

What would He say next? Where would He lead me? My life never was quite the same after I started spending this time with God.

I limited my study to Jesus and the Gospels. The Gospels were familiar to me, as they are to most Christians, but I had also preached and taught them. So, I wanted to approach them from a different perspective.

I decided to study passages that illustrated how Jesus trained His disciples. Instead of the typical study of how Jesus responded to different situations, I decided to examine what the disciples themselves saw and heard. Jesus was, after all, training His disciples. I would be a learner too!

Preface

This journey through the Gospels was a new adventure, full of unique paths that led to unbelievable gardens of new learning. I sat enchanted at Jesus' feet and, vicariously, could see through the disciples' eyes and ears, participating in Jesus' training. I wanted Jesus to disciple me too!

I learned a lot from these times of meditation—in fact, I learned too much if I can say that. My poor mind and heart were overloaded daily with truths and experiences that significantly tested me. This happened so regularly that I became almost scared of what I would learn the next day, knowing it would again overwhelm my emotions and spiritual senses. This book records some of those daily experiences that lasted for several weeks, maybe a month.

As a result of meeting God like this, I cannot doubt that God wants to speak to other Christians similarly. He wants to speak loud and clear so that we can explore the depth of the Gospels. The real question is whether we want Him to speak to us. How desperate are we for Him to speak to us?

Each of my meditation sessions focused on a new passage. I would read and reflect on the selected passage ***until*** He spoke to me through His Word, which would typically require reading the passage once or twice. Most lessons were easy to grasp, but the Lord trained me through other passages, which expanded my faith as I learned to properly read the Bible. These were unique experiences that brought decisive changes to my life.

The more challenging lessons took longer to sink in, but I remained in meditation until at least one truth was unleashed into my soul. I was often tempted to give up and be satisfied with a general reading of His Word, but I finally decided that no matter how long it took, I needed to keep reading the same passage until He spoke to me. Because the Lord had so powerfully built up my faith, I knew He was able and willing to speak to me through any passage in His Word—no matter how familiar the passage was. God could and would speak to me; I only needed to persist. I was not to turn the page or allow my mind to wander off to another passage or situation. I resolved to meditate on the passage that He had directed me to, even if it was chosen in a somewhat unexpected way. I thank the Lord for His extra grace to read the passage until He spoke.

Each session ended with an application for my life. Usually, this was relatively easy. He was present as He taught me, so He used everyday events to imprint the lesson on my life. Many of these I share.

Once God arrested my attention with a passage's truth, I invariably needed to repent. Every passage opened my eyes to another awful aspect of my spiritual condition. I had been a Christian for many years, but the teachings I absorbed during these meditations were so poignant that I often ended up with tears running down my face. I still remember wondering what my children must have thought when they walked by and saw me so moved. (I sat in the same living room chair where I used to listen to the radio broadcast.) But indeed, these meditations were much more than a Bible reading. I met God—or, should I say, God met me—in the deep unknown needs of my heart.

The encounters were remarkable. It was as if the Spirit took me to where the disciples were watching Jesus or asking Him a question. He enabled me to see what Jesus was getting at. Like Paul the Apostle, none of us has yet reached a point of perfection, and I have seen that we have so much more room for spiritual development than we can even think.

> Brethren, I do not regard myself as having laid hold of it yet; but one thing I do: forgetting what lies behind and reaching forward to what lies ahead. (Phil 3:13)

This book records the most poignant lessons I learned in that season of meditation. By reading, I hope you, too, will learn how to hear God speak to you through His Word. When you do, you will experience some of the most tremendous teachings and applications for your life.

Though the Bible was written so long ago, the Lord still wants to speak to you and me. He has already instructed us to meditate in His Word, so put the television, computer games, smartphones, social media, and movies aside. Sit down and challenge Him to speak to you through His Word. He is faithful. Just remember the key: whatever He tells you to do, do it. The daring but necessary heart condition of willingness makes each meditation an adventure with an ending we cannot anticipate.

Paul J. Bucknell
Revised 2023, USA

Introduction

To live fulfilled Christian lives, we must walk with Jesus. Yet, it can be challenging to learn how to walk with Him. Perhaps one reason for this difficulty is our general lack of understanding of the word "abide" in John 15. Jesus uses it naturally, as it was part of his daily experience, but the English translations of "abiding," "remaining," or "living in" do not get at the essence of Jesus' words.

No life, experience, or joy can exceed that which comes from abiding in Christ!

Years ago, thanks to John 15, I wanted to understand grape vines better. Because I was brought up in the city, I had little opportunity to observe them. When I planted three vines in my yard, I had regular opportunities to observe how they grew. My grape vines had thick trunks from which longer and more tender vines stretched out. Jesus uses the vine illustration to illustrate how these tender branches are attached (abide) in the vine's trunk.

They illustrate how we can live rich Christian lives. Abiding is symbolic of attaching to, connecting with, branching from, interworking with, and depending on the Lord; by abiding, we produce juicy, luscious fruit.

> I am the vine, you are the branches; he who abides in Me, and I in him, he bears much fruit; for apart from Me you can do nothing. (John 15:5)

I want to share some of the events I experienced on my journey of learning to abide in Jesus. If you haven't yet joined in this exciting journey, please do. I've summarized some elementary guidelines for this journey below:

- The journey begins by getting to know Jesus. He is alive, having been resurrected from the dead.

- Encounters with Him continually expose our horrible sins. The Holy Spirit causes us to grieve over this sin and wish for it to be removed. We ask and find complete forgiveness through Jesus' work on the cross (1 John 1:9).

- As His disciples, we continue on the strategic path by consistently obeying His commands.

- Once on that path, we need to remain with Jesus. This is the process of "abiding in Christ" from John 15, or, as I have nicknamed it, "walking with Jesus." This lifestyle produces a conscious awareness and dependence upon His presence wherever we go. In the case of the disciples, life was utterly unpredictable and fascinating. Each day was an adventure with Jesus. When we abide in Christ, our relationships, encounters, and life events become uniquely God-arranged.

Come and deepen your understanding by daily walking with Jesus. You can start by reading through the chapters in this book. Or, even better, use the Bible passages included in these chapters to meditate on His Word and only afterward read how He taught me.

He is waiting to meet with you and take you on a beautiful journey. Although you might be brought to tears, you will be glad you chose to meet with Him.

Impossible Love

Mark 8:1-9

In those days again, when there was a great multitude and they had nothing to eat, He called His disciples and said to them, "I feel compassion for the multitude because they have remained with Me now three days, and have nothing to eat; and if I send them away hungry to their home, they will faint on the way; and some of them have come from a distance."

And His disciples answered Him, "Where will anyone be able to find enough to satisfy these men with bread here in a desolate place?" And He was asking them, "How many loaves do you have?" And they said, "Seven." And He directed the multitude to sit down on the ground; and taking the seven loaves, He gave thanks and broke them, and started giving them to His disciples to serve to them, and they served them to the multitude. They also had a few small fish; and after He had blessed them, He ordered these to be served as well. And they ate and were satisfied; and they picked up seven large baskets full of what was left over of the broken pieces. And about four thousand were there; and He sent them away. (Mark 8:1-9)

I have read this story many times. But as much as I read it, I missed the main point just as often.

Perhaps it was because I was too captivated by the miracle itself; whatever the reason, God revealed the main point to me one day, showing me a vivid lesson about abiding in Him.

My initial quest in this series was relatively simple: I wanted God to show me how to abide in Him. When I read, "I feel compassion…," I knew in my heart that He would teach me a powerful lesson on this subject.

The disciples accompanied Jesus that day. They saw what Jesus saw: the large crowd out in a desolate place, intently listening to Jesus' teachings. The teachings were necessary, even life-changing. We know this because they went without food for three days. Though quite unprepared, they camped out so they wouldn't miss anything. They were captivated by Jesus' words. But all things come to an end, and Jesus knew this particular time with the crowd had come to a close. He was undoubtedly tired from teaching God's Word to the people for three days, but He considered their physical needs too.

Did you notice that Jesus operated from love? He thought and felt for their needs. There is no recording of the disciples' thoughts for the crowd, so we don't know whether they were concerned for the crowd or not. But it was clear that Jesus did, and this response set Him apart from the disciples, then and now. Jesus responded to the people's needs, whereas the disciples responded to resources. Jesus knew God's will was to love others. The disciples limited their ministry by what they thought they could do.

After reading this passage, I thought about how often I judged God's will by what I could figure out rather than by what the Lord could do with the heavenly Father's help. Jesus used the resources available—loaves and fish—for the miracle. While Jesus put love into action, the disciples were caught up and focused on their limited resources, "There's no way these few loaves will feed this many people!"

Compassion, not sight, shaped Jesus' faith. He understood that His Father's love extended to these people. Love, after all, is the command above commands because it summarizes every other command. While reflecting on this passage, I realized that I, like the disciples, needed further training in two ways:

- Look for ways to love people.
- Trust God for resources to love them.

George Mueller was a man of faith but also a man of love. In 1835, he started caring for children born out of wedlock and those orphaned. For over ten years, he rented houses to shelter these children. Renting had advantages, as it left more money to invest in kingdom needs. Something happened, though, that changed the course of his thinking.

On October 30, 1845, he received a letter from a man living on the same street where the four orphanages were located. It was a kind and friendly letter, but he stated how the Orphan Houses inconvenienced the people of Wilson Street. He left the affair in Mueller's hands.

Mr. Mueller had had no thought or desire to build for ten years. But he began to think differently about his situation when he received the letter from his neighbor. He wrote down the pros and cons of moving or not. In the end, he discerned that it was God's will to move. The primary reason was the inconvenience to the neighbors. Philippians 4:5 affirmed this for him. "Let your forbearing spirit (yieldingness) be known to all men. The Lord is near."

He felt a great responsibility for the noise the children made and the abuse of the sewage system (houses weren't built for so many occupants). He tried to think of other solutions but could not think of any. Others confirmed he should build. After praying for a season, George sensed God was using this occasion to demonstrate His love to the neighbors and better provide for the children. Behind all this was Mr. Mueller's desire to see people know of God's great and glorious work.

One might think little of this situation except that George had no money in hand to build. By conviction, he did not ask for funds. Furthermore, he would not go into debt. And to buy a place big enough for 300 children was an impossibility. Anyone could decide to do something, but in George's case, where would the funds come from? However, like Jesus, Mr. Mueller did not live by the resources he possessed but by what God would provide.

Is this not the pattern we saw when Jesus fed the 4,000 men plus their families? Mr. Mueller estimated the cost back then:

- 2,000-3,000 pounds for property (6-7 acres) around Bristol, England
- 6,000-8,000 pounds for a building (lower estimate)
- 1,500 pounds for bare furnishings for the 300-400 people using the building.

He said:

> This is indeed a large sum of money that I need; but my hope is in God. I have not sought after this thing; it has not begun with me. God has altogether unexpectedly, by means of the letter before mentioned, led me to it. Only the day before I received the letter, I had no more thought about building premises for the accommodation of the orphans than I had had during the ten previous years.[1]

Love and the glory of God shaped his thinking and firmed up his decision to start on this project. Without asking anybody for the finances, 15,784 pounds came in, and after everything was built and cared for, there remained a balance of 776 pounds. From the day he began asking the Lord for the building to the day it was completed was 1,195 days. Three hundred orphans were cared for in the new orphanage on Ashley Down.

I am amazed at how similar this story is to the one where Jesus fed the multitude. Love should dictate our decisions rather than our resources. We must be need-focused rather than resource-focused.

---

[1] Story taken from *Autobiography of George Müller*, edited by Wayland (pp. 294 ff.).

Our walk with Jesus will primarily be made up of miracles. We do not have what it takes to meet the needs of the people and situations God brings us. Whether it begs for healing, wisdom, direction, power, etc., we are to let love move us into faith and let God work out the details while we watch!

Genuine Friendship

John 15:15-16

No longer do I call you slaves, for the slave does not know what his master is doing; but I have called you friends, for all things that I have heard from My Father I have made known to you. You did not choose Me, but I chose you, and appointed you, that you should go and bear fruit, and [that] your fruit should remain, that whatever you ask of the Father in My name, He may give to you. (John 15:15-16)

I have always longed for deep friendship, a fact that I am embarrassed to have discovered in the middle of my life. It is not that I have no friends; I have had many friends in different seasons of my life. But I long for and thoroughly enjoy deep friendships.

Perhaps my father's absence in my early years deepened my longing for deep friendships. As I began to explore the depth of my relationship with God, I asked Him to teach me how to foster deeper friendships. I didn't quite know how to pursue a father-son relationship with Him—after all, it had not been modeled for me.

I was surprised that one of the first steps in becoming more intimate with Jesus was for Him to teach me about friendship.

Fortunately, the penetrating message didn't take long to sink deep into my friendship-craving heart. The Lord was to be my friend, not just my master. I sensed the Lord's fabulous presence as I thought through these penetrating messages. Two messages came to me loud and clear:

A friend accepts you as you are.

A friend likes to spend time with you.

Upon pondering this later statement, I was humbled. I realized that though I spent time with Him, He wanted to spend even more time with me. In this case, He urged me to stop listening to an afternoon radio program so that I could spend more focused time with Him. I could sense a strong tension in my soul. It was hard for me to slow down and spend more time being friends.

I determined that a close relationship with God is what I desired. I thought more about how my childhood difficulties had shaped my desire for deep intimacy. He created a deep longing and kindly filled it with His glorious presence. I committed to follow up and pursue more deliberate and concentrated times with Him alone.

Later that afternoon, I found myself reading an article on spiritual intimacy in my study. As I was reading, one of my sons came to my study to review his math with me. He was having trouble with a problem. After reviewing the question, I couldn't understand the instructions in his second-grade book either. I told him to do the understandable part of the problem and ignore the rest. I guess my suggestion was too nonconformist. He couldn't accept my words. I wanted to read the article on intimacy, but my son was disturbing me. Without the issue coming to a resolution, I soon sent him from my study until he could compose himself.

The Spirit of God was already working in my heart during this scene. I could see the Lord's displeasure with me. Here I was, trying to spend time with the Lord, but I couldn't even patiently teach and guide my son. The verse from 1 Corinthians 13 convicted me: "Love is patient."

My heart was humbled. I didn't want my Heavenly Father to treat me like I had just treated my son! I repented to God and my son when I realized that it was not right for me to treat either of them in this way. God clearly taught me, "A friend likes to spend time with a friend." I needed to be a true friend to those around me, which meant I must spend time with those I claimed to love.

The Lord didn't waste a second. Not long after the math situation was resolved, my nine-year-old daughter entered my study. I could tell something was wrong. She told me that she didn't go out with the others to invite the neighborhood children to next week's Bible Club. The Holy Spirit prompted me that this was another opportunity to spend extra time with someone—to be a friend. So I ignored my reading, which was very difficult for me, and I, like Jesus would have done, spent time with my daughter. This turned out to be the most meaningful conversation I ever had with her!

She had been having lots of trouble with fear, so I began to share from the scriptures where the Lord told her not to fear and worry. At first, she didn't want to pray, but after I prayed for her and freed her mind to think clearly, she was willing. She repeated a repentance and forgiveness prayer after me, line by line. I then asked her in a prayerful spirit to share what fears were on her heart. After a moment, she said the fear of sickness and embarrassment. After this prayer and further conversation about salvation, she left free and happy as a lark. God had taken away her long-standing stomachache. God had delivered her from the fears that oppressed her.

I am thankful I took that time to be with my daughter instead of chasing her out of my study to guard my privacy. By God's grace, I try to give that particular focus to each person I meet so that I might discern whether the Lord wants to give any special love to them. I need so much help in this area, but what an exciting beginning!

A friend must be a friend. When walking with Jesus, I need to pause to spend extra time with Him. I also need to look out for the people God brings into my life. He might want me to be a friend to them, even when I'm busy with another task.

A Vial of Love

Mark 14:1-9

Now the Passover and Unleavened Bread was two days off; and the chief priests and the scribes were seeking how to seize Him by stealth, and kill Him; for they were saying, "Not during the festival, lest there be a riot of the people." And while He was in Bethany at the home of Simon the leper, and reclining at the table, there came a woman with an alabaster vial of very costly perfume of pure nard; and she broke the vial and poured it over His head.

But some were indignantly remarking to one another, "Why has this perfume been wasted? For this perfume might have been sold for over three hundred denarii, and the money given to the poor." And they were scolding her. But Jesus said, "Let her alone; why do you bother her? She has done a good deed to Me. For the poor you always have with you, and whenever you wish, you can do them good; but you do not always have Me. She has done what she could; she has anointed My body beforehand for the burial. And truly I say to you, wherever the gospel is preached in the whole world, that also which this woman has done shall be spoken of in memory of her." (Mark 14:1-9)

Our walk with Jesus must not be so focused on ministry that we forget that the most significant part of being a Christian is knowing Christ! This can be such a challenging lesson for us. We work so hard to provide money for our family that, in the end, we don't spend much time with them. We work so hard to prepare a Sunday school lesson that we forget that we need to be personally enriched by God's Word first. It is not uncommon that a **task** diminishes the importance of our **relationship** with God.

God designed the Sabbath so we would not be ruled by our tasks/work. Our relationship with God is to take priority over our work. God wants us to slow down sufficiently to enjoy things. More importantly, He wants us to enjoy being with Him.

As teachers or preachers of God's word, we can so easily stress reading the Bible, studying the Bible, and memorizing the Bible that we forget the real intent of good spiritual disciplines—which is to be so caught up in the truths of scripture that we can do nothing but adore our Lord.

I used to ask people whether or not they had devotions that day. By asking after their devotions, I meant to ask whether they had had a great time with the Lord in His Word and prayer. I now realize that many people thought I was asking whether they had read the Bible or prayed. They missed the idea that "having devotions" meant meeting the Lord. The activity isn't as important as the meeting with the Lord. This doesn't mean we can do without prayer and meditation—God has ordained the use of these things to meet Him—however, the means must not become the end!

Mark 14:1-9 A Vial of Love

This passage beautifully displays how devotion goes levels beyond the mere exercise of religious duties.

Mary was so deeply devoted to Jesus that she took a precious —if not her most precious—possession and poured it over Him.[2] This event revealed an overwhelming spirit of thankfulness and joy in Mary's heart to know Jesus' blessings. I am sure she thought of her brother Lazarus' resurrection, but we know from the account of Luke 10:38-42 that her passionate devotion and love for Him were evident even before that epic event.

After pondering this story, my heart was moved to give my Lord whatever He wanted in my life. I thought of the most valuable treasure I had. Was it my money? I didn't have much. My van? My house? My family? My heart? Earlier in my life, I had given these things, one by one, to the Lord. All that I have and am, including my life, reputation, wife, children, wealth, and possessions, I had given to Him.

In a quiet sense of joy, through the stirring account of Mary, I again dedicated the most precious thing to Him—my heart. He is my all in all. I have nothing that is mine. All is His.

Abiding means spending time with. To be clear, this is not ministry time. Jesus wants to be alone with us. I want to be alone with Him. We all need to be deliberate about this. Mary and the other disciples loved the quiet time spent with Jesus, enjoying His presence. Only those who loved His

---

[2] See John 12 for the parallel story.

presence were there. Not long afterward, Jesus would head down the valley and ascend Jerusalem's mountain to die on the cross and be rejected and abandoned by all.

Abiding with Jesus will cost us the things we most treasure. For Mary, this was her costly perfume. For me, it was my life and my loved ones. One powerful incident happened seven years earlier. God asked me for my loved ones, but in an odd way. Let me explain.

I was taking a shower early one Sunday morning, preparing for church before anyone else was awake. With my preaching duties, it would be a typical busy Sunday.

I experienced a sudden pain in my chest that made breathing difficult. I quickly got out of the shower, dried, dressed, and went to my study to pray. This ongoing pain might be signaling the end of my life. I might be dying.

In an intensive time of prayer, kneeling on the floor, and speaking with the Lord, I entrusted my family and ministry to the Lord. I was weeping, still on the floor, as I said a possible goodbye to my wife and children, but in my very intense prayer I dedicated each of them to the Lord. In a sense, they were no longer mine but the Lord's. I was ready to go to be with Him. As it happened, I went to the emergency room later that night, but they could not find any genuine heart problem with all their tests. A spray of nitroglycerin took any subsiding pain away. My time now belongs to God. I had given my treasured loved ones to Him.

Abiding in Christ is costly. Love is costly. Love requires us to use all we have to pursue the needs of others. The perfume vial seemed like a strange offering, but it represented Mary's view of what was most important. The perfume she offered could have been sold at any time to support her during an emergency. With the bottle emptied, though, her safety net was gone. The grandeur of having a robust and mystic scent in her possession no longer enchanted her. She had something much more significant; Jesus was hers. He was real. He belonged to her, and she belonged to Him.

Following is Not Easy

Mark 10:46-52

And they came to Jericho. And as He was going out from Jericho with His disciples and a great multitude, a blind beggar named Bartimaeus, the son of Timaeus, was sitting by the road. And when he heard that it was Jesus the Nazarene, he began to cry out and say, "Jesus, Son of David, have mercy on me!" And many were sternly telling him to be quiet, but he kept crying out all the more, "Son of David, have mercy on me!" And Jesus stopped and said, "Call him here." And they called the blind man, saying to him, "Take courage, arise! He is calling for you." And casting aside his cloak, he jumped up, and came to Jesus. And answering him, Jesus said, "What do you want Me to do for you?" And the blind man said to Him, "Rabboni, I want to regain my sight!" And Jesus said to him, "Go your way; your faith has made you well." And immediately he regained his sight and began following Him on the road. (Mark 10:46-52)

We're not so different from the folks in the crowd. They were insensitive to the blind man, some even daring to hush him to silence. Maybe they were trying to shield their Master from annoyance. However, the more I read this story, the more I could relate to those my soul inwardly scolded.

Likewise, I would have enjoyed walking with the crowd and Jesus, and I, too, would have minimized the needs of someone on the fringe. I may not have been one of those who tried to silence the blind beggar, but I also would not have tried to draw Jesus' attention to the needs of the blind man.

I do my best to develop ways that help me stay as close to Jesus as possible. After all, My life had been transformed. Like the others following Jesus, He has lavishly blessed me too. Jesus Christ had been very good to me. I can't think of why it would be wrong for the disciples to want to retain that closeness to Him. By shunning the blind man, they would somewhat protect Jesus from all the requests and remain by His side.

So why did Jesus stop? Had I been in that crowd, I wonder if I would have even heard that man's cry for help. It was then that I discovered I was more like the crowd than I'd imagined. I wanted Jesus to be with me; I didn't want Him to be with others.

Our definition of follower seems to be more along the lines of, "I like to be near You" rather than "I want to be like You." The crowd stopped when Jesus called and waited for Bartimaeus.

Even though they had initially told the man to be quiet, I am sure they were happy for him when Jesus healed him. Jesus' amazing miracle enabled this blind man, though rejected by his well-known and highly respected father Timaeus,[3] to follow Jesus. I would be happy for him, too. But why don't I look out for people seeking Jesus and try to make a way to introduce them to Him?

Most of us get caught up in the minutiae of our relationships with Jesus and become unfaithful disciples because we aren't focusing on becoming more like Jesus. How many took the time to care for this poor, rejected soul?

Each of us has the opportunity to either be near Jesus (association) or become more like him (to follow him). Bartimaeus had his opportunity too. Would he be infected with the spiritual elitism of the crowd or run to the needy people crying out for help? Would he get caught up in a parade of spiritual pride or focus on the need to distribute God's goodness to as many as God willed? This question remains one that each of us needs to consider seriously.

We must be prepared to go where Jesus goes. Our friendship with Him is not perfectly equal. We are friends, but He is Lord. He leads; we follow.

My oldest boy typically ran ahead of us during our walks when he was young—to lead us, in a sense. But there were a few times when, once he turned around to find the rest of

---

[3] Timaeus literally means "highly prized." We can safely presume that Timaeus was well respected and honored. In the Biblical context, this also usually means that he was well off. If this was so, we can gather that Bartimaeus was rejected by his family because of his blindness and had to beg for his food. ["Bar" means "son of," so "Bartimaeus" means "son of Timaeus."] We can surmise the rejection of his family; it seems the crowd knew and rejected him too.

us, he saw us going in a different direction! I sense that this is how many treat our relationship with Jesus. An honest reading of this account is jarring—it shows how I delude myself, assuming I am close to Him, when in reality, He has turned aside to care for some needy soul.

My mistakes are more common than my successes. One day, when down at the city park with my children, I saw an older lady oddly sprawled out on a park bench. She was dressed in many clothes—more than you would expect in the heat of a summer day. My conscience pricked me, urging me to go over and see if she needed any help. "Jesus would have talked with her," I can remember thinking. My children were swinging on their own at that point, so my conscience finally won. I went over and talked with her. It turns out, she was resting before climbing up the nearby hill, which evidently led to her home. It was a pleasant chat. But that is what scared me: we hadn't had a deep enough conversation to indicate she had some real need or whether she was interested in knowing Jesus.

She didn't see Jesus in me. She didn't meet up with His love because I had not been willing to engage on a deeper level. And, even worse, I was willing to leave her alone on a park bench while I played with my children. As I thought about it later, I realized that Jesus would have pursued her further to see if she needed help. It would have taken only a few words to say, "Can I help you in some way?" or "Is there any particular need I could pray for?"

> My mind was elsewhere because my heart was elsewhere.
> I didn't care.

I had to repent from focusing on my own needs. There I was, abounding in God's marvelous grace, intent on enjoying Christ's riches by myself. I was so rich yet uncaring toward the real poor. Later, I noticed that she had gone. I stood condemned on that playground. I hadn't seen her go; she was not in my heart. But it wasn't only the woman on the bench who had left. My opportunity to be a minister of Jesus also disappeared.

I lifted a prayer in the spirit of Psalm 143:2: "And do not enter into judgment with Thy servant, for in Thy sight no man living is righteous."

My failure rate climbed in my new quest to follow Jesus. I saw more clearly just how much I still needed His grace and ask for His mercy. My sin of neglect seemed more significant than my experience of His incredible love at that moment.

I want to say that I am like Jesus and follow and love Him. This claim, however, is now seasoned with much more humility. Every day I humbly ask Him to take my hand and lead me because I am the blind one. It can be so difficult to respond to the Spirit's prompting to minister to those around me, those whom Jesus sees and cares for.

Listening Carefully

Mark 7:17-18

And when leaving the multitude, He had entered the house, His disciples questioned Him about the parable. And He said to them, "Are you so lacking in understanding also? Do you not understand that whatever goes into the man from outside cannot defile him?" (Mark 7:17-18)

Can we ever learn too much? I don't think so. However, we can learn the wrong things, which can cause a dense fog to form over our minds and keep us from learning the right things with the right spirit.

I have become more aware of a mist that often seeps over my mind each time I sit down to read God's Word. Out of the mist comes a few thoughts: "You already know this." "Good thing you don't have to study this again." "Don't you have something better to do?" But something changed upon reading Jesus' word in the following passage: "Are you so lacking in understanding also?" (Mark 7:17).

I don't know what it was. Maybe some old stubbornness resurfaced, presenting a more significant challenge as I walked with the Lord. Whatever it was, this insight was beneficial to me.

I am confident that the Lord wants me to sit next to Him so I can listen to Him speak to me. Those distracting suggestions visit my mind, but God's Spirit disperses them and reminds me of my commitment to be serious with Him while I'm meditating.

It's scary to think of how many times I have sat down and not profited from the scriptures because of the absence of my good desires to love and cherish God and His Word. I am afraid there have been thousands of lost opportunities. Of course, I have had great times in God's Word. All has not been lost. Without knowing it, I plowed into God's Word and came out with a tremendous gain. But there are too many times when the words of Jesus, "Are you too so uncomprehending?" have directly applied to my life.

We might interpret Jesus' statement, "Are you so lacking in understanding also?" as rather unfair. After all, how long had the disciples been with Jesus anyway? Yet Jesus was compassionate; He is compassionate still. His love for His disciples did not stop. Jesus was not haughty but displayed great care for His disciples in three compassionate thoughts.

• What is holding you back from learning?

Jesus identifies their lack of zeal to know God's truth. Jesus would not have rebuked them if they had been unable to comprehend these truths earlier. They had their chances. I, too, have had my chances.

Was it because I was not seeking? Not believing? Not wanting? Was there too much pride in my heart? Those questions kept me from genuine heart-learning.

Jesus knew they had the opportunity for better and more prosperous lives if only they would store God's Word in their hearts, just as Mary treasured the words the angel brought to her when announcing Jesus' conception (Luke 2:19).

• What will happen when I am not with you?

Time is short. If you flip through a few pages in the Gospel, you will read about Jesus' crucifixion. And if you jump a few short months ahead, we would read of Jesus' body wrapped and placed in a tomb. Were the disciples ready? They weren't.

We see this most vividly when the disciples all turned aside and left Jesus alone to be hung on the cruel cross. The truths of God's Word had not properly penetrated their hearts. The best test to see how deeply God's Word has affected us is to observe how much His words influence our thoughts and decisions during crises.

Are God's truths with you, or have you thrown them aside, as though they have no relevance to your life? Jesus knew the disciples would fall if they were not strengthened. Indeed, they did fall.

- **Will you be able to take my truth and properly minister to others?**

They were able to teach. They had heard the most incredible teachings from the Greatest Teacher. They heard lots of sermons and illustrations straight from the Master's lips.

But had God's truth touched their hearts deeply enough to light their souls on fire? Were His teachings so alive that just the memory of them would keep their hearts focused on the needs and concerns of others? A little truth is a dangerous thing. A wrong perspective of truth can be lethal. Pride not only keeps us from caring for others but can also hurt them. Jesus wanted to work in their lives so that they could help others.

How can we get beyond the accepted theological grids and systems that keep essential truths from our lives?

Do I also need more understanding? Yes. Like the disciples, I, too, have just enough truth to keep the truth from me. We tend to create filters in our minds or form groups of assumptions that keep the deeper truths of God out of our minds (I call these "theological grids"). We are so influenced by what people say that we have great difficulty understanding the truth.

The disciples accompanied Jesus, but this didn't improve the situation! They needed to ask Jesus. It was easy to take pride in their association with God's Holy Savior yet remain spiritually blind.

Could I, too, be so uncomprehending, even after years of exposure to His precious truth? Has my walk likewise become stale? My heart was saddened to think about how close I could have been to Him if only I had understood His words. The blame rests with me, not others. My cold heart was what kept me away. A dark, penetrating mist would have had little effect if my heart genuinely longed for Him. I confessed my sin and denounced my stale attachment to the living Word of God.

But how can I be sure Jesus will keep making His truth alive? I might fall into the same pattern again! My prayer is that the work that He started will continue. "For I am confident of this very thing, that He who began a good work in you will perfect it until the day of Christ Jesus" (Phil 1:6).

Jesus is the framework through which I view His Word. He is there right beside me. I need to keep my attention on Him and sincerely ask Him what He wants me to learn. I need to listen to Him today, tomorrow, and always. In my time with Him, I know I can bring any concern before Him. Sometimes He even uses the scripture passage I meditate on to provide answers to impossible situations.

Jesus cared for His disciples, and He greatly desires that all of us would continue to keep our hearts open to His truth! He genuinely cares about our spiritual welfare, our growth, and the ministry of our lives. What might we miss out on if we don't cultivate openness to Him? Everything.

Abiding in Jesus means listening to what He says.

A Faith that Counts

Mark 11:20-24

And as they were passing by in the morning, they saw the fig tree withered from the roots up. And being reminded, Peter said to Him, "Rabbi, behold, the fig tree which You cursed has withered." And Jesus answered saying to them, "Have faith in God. Truly I say to you, whoever says to this mountain, 'Be taken up and cast into the sea,' and does not doubt in his heart, but believes that what he says is going to happen, it shall be granted him. "Therefore I say to you, all things for which you pray and ask, believe that you have received them, and they shall be granted you." (Mark 11:20-24)

I often wonder if, by hanging around with Jesus, certain things will rub off on me. This phenomenon often happens when we spend a lot of time with friends. We mimic their expressions and attitudes and even make similar conclusions and decisions. When I hear one of my older children say something a certain way, I can instantly "hear" how similar it is to his friend's expression.

This passage helped me realize how desperate I once was. I remember visiting Indianapolis. I forget why I was there, but while there, I received a revelation in my prayer life. It is somewhat embarrassing, but I'll tell you anyway. I realized that it is not uncommon for me to ask the Lord for things yet fail to have faith that He will genuinely answer.

I was shocked. Were these prayers that lacked faith wasteful? Jesus doesn't mention whether prayers without faith are of no value, but if the purpose of asking is to get, something is missing! I sensed that I needed to start praying in faith. I needed to ask for a larger dining room table. Our growing family could no longer easily fit around our table. I prayed, asked, and believed, or so I thought. Whenever I talked to our children on the phone while in Indianapolis, I asked them if anything special had happened. "Everything is fine," they would say. When I returned home, I was disappointed that we had not received a larger dining room table.

Some might say we don't need to pray for such needs, but I would maintain that we do. We ought to bring our needs to the Lord in prayer. Jesus said three things that indicate that praying for material things like tables is appropriate:

- In one of his teachings, Jesus cursed a fig tree, and the following day it withered as a result of his curse. This serves as a reminder that our prayers are not restricted to intangible things. Through this miracle, Jesus imparted a spiritual lesson. Similarly, I prayed for a table to teach my children a spiritual lesson.

- Second, we have Jesus' extreme example of telling a mountain to be taken up and cast into the sea. I see absolutely no spiritual significance in this illustration, either. It only emphasizes that the content of the prayer is not as important as the faith.

- Third, we note Jesus' words, "all things." This emphasizes that He is not speaking merely about spiritual matters but includes all life matters. Our faith is what makes things spiritual.

Because we did not get a new, big dining room table, I concluded that I didn't believe.[4] I doubted. Jesus could not have spoken more clearly on these matters. As a sound technician, He pinpoints where the problems lie.

By God's grace, however, I have seen answers to prayer. My faith, or the lack thereof, was thus not shaken. It was a good lesson. The disappointing factor in all of it was how quickly I forgot about my newly found discovery—that faith is key to prayer. I went right back to dull, ineffective, and faithless prayers where I just asked and did not believe.

This passage in Mark woke me up once again and stimulated me to review my experiences of prayer and faith and their results. At one point, my church was hoping and praying for a huge turnout for an evangelistic meeting. I sat down next to a hardworking coworker at the beginning of the meeting. Not many had come. He labored and prepared many supplies, praying hard for the meeting and its attendees. I felt pity for him. It was as if the Spirit of the Lord came upon me and gave me the faith to believe that, though fewer were in attendance than we had hoped, we would still see many hearts turn to the Lord. I believed and, with my brother, we saw the fruits of those prayers.

---

[4] I learned that I could misread His will. Obviously, this was not a God-generated faith but a self-generated hope—not faith.

A study on Elijah, Abraham, and other figures in the Bible will help clarify the nature of faith. Look for an answer to the question, "Where does faith come from?" Here are four points to consider as you get started; I sense they are interrelated:

- Faith comes from abiding in God's presence.
- Faith is a special anointing from God.
- Faith comes by training.
- Faith is a step-by-step process; one's faith must grow.

I had to confess my inadequate faith and cried out for more faith. The issue of the dining room table faded into the background—we could eat while seated on the floor if we had to. It was more important that my prayers be filled with faith, pleasing and glorifying our good God.

Staying Focused on God's Will

Matthew 15:21-28

And Jesus went away from there, and withdrew into the district of Tyre and Sidon. And behold, a Canaanite woman came out from that region, and began to cry out, saying, "Have mercy on me, O Lord, Son of David; my daughter is cruelly demon-possessed." But He did not answer her a word. And His disciples came to Him and kept asking Him, saying, "Send her away, for she is shouting out after us." But He answered and said, "I was sent only to the lost sheep of the house of Israel." But she came and began to bow down before Him, saying, "Lord, help me!" And He answered and said, "It is not good to take the children's bread and throw it to the dogs." But she said, "Yes, Lord; but even the dogs feed on the crumbs which fall from their masters' table." Then Jesus answered and said to her, "O woman, your faith is great; be it done for you as you wish." And her daughter was healed at once. (Matt 15:21-28)

Have you ever tried to help someone only to discover that your help wasn't appreciated? In this passage, the disciples were caught in a sort of tug-of-war—they were trying to help Jesus get away from the crowds as He desired, but He wouldn't fully cooperate with their efforts! He had journeyed with His disciples to a distant city outside Israel called Tyre. He told His disciples not to tell anyone else where He was staying.[5] He wanted a quiet retreat, a time to be spiritually close to God and alone with His disciples. However, as in real life, Jesus found His planned retreat interrupted.

I remember vividly one morning of interruption in my home office. Admittedly, my office is more prone to invasion than the average office building, but neither is impervious to distractions.

One child requested my attention, and after resolving the issue, I kindly asked him to close the door on his way out and not to disturb me. Another child came with the same question, however. Again, I was interrupted! Then they started to loudly play one of their children's songs/stories on their radio, so I went down the hallway, asked them to turn it down, and closed their door, telling them that I was trying to study.

This conveyor belt of distraction went on for about fifteen minutes (I'm still surprised at how much I managed to get done). I finally wedged an extra chair against the door, desperate for some quiet! But then another, a third child, the two-year-old, came by and pushed the door hard, causing the chair to slide from its place just a bit. After noticing the chair there, he retreated rather quickly. He had never seen

---

[5] "And from there He arose and went away to the region of Tyre. And when He had entered a house, He wanted no one to know of it; yet He could not escape notice" (Mark 7:24). The parallel passage is Mark 7:24-30.

me so desperate for quiet time that I would place a big chair against the door!

Jesus was in this Canaanite land to find quiet. His healing ministry in Israel caused great commotion wherever He went. The religious leaders were beginning to be antagonistic and expressed resistance to the God they pledged to love. But no matter why Jesus was there, He always did His Father's will. His disciples were slower to learn, however.

We should first note this woman's persistent faith. No matter how many obstacles were in her way, she persisted. The disciples were not being helpful here: "Send her away!" But Jesus was not too concerned to stick to the plan either. The difference between the disciples and Jesus is stark: the disciples chose the lesser goal of being alone, whereas Jesus chose to serve. The disciples were blinded to God's greater plan and will. They did not understand that God might have sent them such a distance to meet this particular person's needs.

Jesus was willing to let the situation play out. He knew His primary goal was to be alone and refreshed, but He was always open to doing His Father's will—even when it was inconvenient.

I'm not trying to comment on whether this decision was hard or easy for Jesus. Usually, when getting away, we enter a relaxation mode and begin unwinding. One would expect Jesus to ignore the request or heal the daughter and send her away, since His goal was to rest. He could have quickly healed this woman's afflicted daughter if He wished.

How did Jesus test whether or not this was a real need from the Father or just another disruption in His life? Jesus responded four times to the woman's persistent pleading.

- First, Jesus remained silent. He said nothing. The first test was to ascertain real needs. If a person seeking help becomes quiet, they need no special care.

- Second, Jesus stated His mission, "I was sent only to the lost sheep of the house of Israel." Jesus analyzed the request in light of the mission God had sent Him on. In this case, Jesus stated that He was sent to His people, the Jews.[6] Jesus was very mission-conscious. The woman understood this, but it didn't stop her.

- Third, Jesus tested her faith. He was sent to minister to Israel specifically. By speaking of God's grace to Israel, God's children, He excluded her, a foreigner, from God's goodness. "It is not good to take the children's bread and throw it to the dogs." The woman's deep faith, humility, and willingness to accept help were evident in her response when she said, "Yes, Lord; but even the dogs eat the crumbs that fall from their masters' table." Her words were full of meaning and showed her desperation for assistance.

---

[6] John 1:11, "He came to His own, and those who were His own did not receive Him." Romans 1:16, "For I am not ashamed of the gospel, for it is the power of God for salvation to everyone who believes, to the Jew first and also to the Greek."

- Last, we note Jesus' clear affirmation of her faith and His announcement that her daughter's suffering caused by severe demonic oppression would be ended, "O woman, your faith is great; be it done for you as you wish." Jesus was poised to rest, but His delight was to care for the people God His Father sent to Him, no matter what He was doing.

Consider this testimony on discerning God's will. A man, Bruce, had a full schedule. At a meeting, he met with a few representatives from South Africa. They asked him to develop some material on AIDS. Bruce quickly said, "No." He knew he was far too busy, and this task did not fit into the ministry God had given him. He knew these guys would go back and tell others to pray.

They met again the following year and repeated their question. They said that they knew he was the right person to do it. But again, even though he was a bit more reflective this time, Bruce refused the request, reiterating that writing the material was not the ministry God had called him to. They stated again that they would pray. Bruce knew they would.

He was confident that this request was outside God's purpose for him. The following year they met again, and they asked him again. He was ready to say no to these guys again, but something happened. Bruce began weeping as the men spoke of the project and the need. A tremendous, unexpected, and deep compassion for these people filled his heart. He knew that God had called him to develop these materials even though it was outside his specific ministry focus, and God was faithful to help him develop the materials despite his busy schedule.[7]

While we must steadily focus on fulfilling our missions, ministries, present responsibilities, and duties, we must always be ready for exceptions. As Jesus' disciples, we might be disgruntled with a person's persistent requests—whether we're on vacation, at a spiritual retreat, or are just plain tired sitting in our backyard. We need to be alert and receptive to interruptions. At the same time, we should not easily give up our God-given missions.

When the desperate faith of another person becomes apparent and is confirmed in our spirits, we should know our Heavenly Father has sent them and will give us all the extraordinary grace to meet their particular need.

****

Dealing with Demands on our Schedules

The graphic below should give us a better understanding of God's purposes for our lives. Ideally, all our present responsibilities should stay within God's overall purpose in the world and the specific purpose He's made us for. Our mission/vision is God's purpose for our lives.

---

[7] From Bruce Wilkinson's seminar talk on the "Beginning of a Vision."

Concentric ovals diagram: outer "God's overall *purpose*", middle "Our mission/*vision*", inner "Present Responsibilities".

A godly response to such challenges to our daily routines would mimic Jesus' response. Two examples include Jesus' visit to Tyre (above) and His ministry to the Samaritan woman (John 4).

God, however, sometimes calls us to be involved in activities outside our customarily understood "mission" or responsibilities. Jesus' response to the Canaanite woman reflected His flexibility, patience, and ability to test her challenging demand, demonstrating how He trusted God to meet her need. He reveals that although He honors his commitment to a schedule and plans, the will of God takes precedence.

Discover Your True Treasure

Mark 10:21-27

And looking at him, Jesus felt a love for him, and said to him, "One thing you lack: go and sell all you possess, and give to the poor, and you shall have treasure in heaven; and come, follow Me." But at these words his face fell, and he went away grieved, for he was one who owned much property. And Jesus, looking around, said to His disciples, "How hard it will be for those who are wealthy to enter the kingdom of God!" And the disciples were amazed at His words.

But Jesus answered again and said to them, "Children, how hard it is to enter the kingdom of God! It is easier for a camel to go through the eye of a needle than for a rich man to enter the kingdom of God." And they were even more astonished and said to Him, "Then who can be saved?" Looking upon them, Jesus said, "With men it is impossible, but not with God; for all things are possible with God." (Mark 10:21-27)

Jesus' disciples made an important discovery that day. This account shows that, at first, they were "amazed" but later became "even more astonished." Our walk with Jesus leads us to various life discoveries; in this case, the disciples' discovery greatly impacted their lives.

So what led to this fantastic discovery that greatly influenced the disciples' lives? A rich man asked Jesus how to inherit eternal life. We cannot know his motive, but let us assume that he wondered whether or not he had done enough to gain eternal life. Jesus didn't question the earnest belief of this man's obedience to the commands that He listed in the preceding verses.

It was love that led Jesus to expose the real issue. "One thing you lack," Jesus said. He commanded the rich man to give all his wealth to charity. This one deed was not a small thing. The wealthy man hadn't had a problem obeying the commands Jesus earlier identified.

Jesus confronted the man's disobedience to the first command, which was to worship only the Lord God. The rich man went away grieved and, at least at that point, unwilling to destroy his heart's true and treasured idol: his wealth. This indeed troubled the disciples' hearts as it does ours. But it led to one of the most surprising discoveries in their lives.

The disciples were amazed at how Jesus broadened this issue to apply to all wealthy people rather than just this one man. Jesus said that all wealthy people would have difficulty entering the kingdom of God, not just this one man. It was as though His disciples could suddenly see a new religion called "Wealth" that could surround the souls of those who did not need to worry about how their daily needs would be met.

Many of us feel this problem of wealth is only a problem for rich people. However, there are many different ways to define wealth and affluence, depending on the context in which we live. For some, not having a connection to the internet is poor. Others do not know where tomorrow's food will come from (in which case, internet access is neither here nor there). I prefer the definition of wealth as having enough so that it's not necessary to be concerned about the next day's physical needs. This definition classifies many of us as wealthy!

Does Jesus mean that wealth is always a great hindrance that keeps people from coming to know the Lord? Does He mean that there is a religion called "wealth" in the modern world, running virtually undetected to Christians? But Jesus did not stop there. He raised the stakes.

Jesus went from speaking about this class of wealthy people to speaking of all men. Jesus said, "Children, how hard it is to enter the kingdom of God!" Jesus made a blanket statement about the difficulties any person might face to become His follower. He seems to do this for several reasons:

- Jesus did not want to imply that only rich people have a problem being saved.
- Jesus warns us of idols, which keep us from God.
- Jesus wanted the disciples to know that human effort can't bring anyone into the kingdom of God.

Consider how we try to make becoming a Christian easy—pray the sinner's prayer, raise a hand. These actions are only helpful if they signify a much more profound change of heart. It just can't be done in one's own power.

Jesus went on to speak about the rich man again, but this time He changed the "hard" language into "impossible." "It is easier for a camel to go through the eye of a needle than for a rich man to enter the kingdom of God."

This elicited an even more extreme response from the disciples. A needle is tiny, and its hole is even more negligible. The camel is a large animal designed to hold a significant amount of water to survive in arid places. Jesus used an impossible example[8] to illustrate the divine aspect of salvation. (In John 3, Jesus uses "born from above" or "born again"—both translations are valid, emphasizing this divine aspect.)

The disciples' response reflects what Jesus tried to convey: "They were even more astonished and said to Him, 'Then who can be saved?'" Only God can change a heart.

Following Jesus always requires God's divine work on the human heart. Faith and repentance are gifts from God. Faith is from God. "For by grace you have been saved through faith; and that not of yourselves, it is the gift of God; not as a result of works, that no one should boast" (Eph 2:8-9). Repentance is from God: "And when they heard this, they quieted down, and glorified God, saying, 'Well then, God has granted to the Gentiles also the repentance [that leads]

---

[8] There are other interpretations of this passage. A simple word and context study shows that it means an actual needle. If the needle referred to some gate, then the term would translate into a name. However, Luke uses a medical term for surgical needle not found elsewhere in the New Testament (Robertson's Word Pictures). Furthermore, the context reveals that the disciples rightly concluded the situation to be impossible.

to life'" (Acts 11:18). Salvation can never be worked for, whether by gifts of charity, religiosity, or avoiding trouble. Jesus stated this clearly.

Man's evil heart wants to cover up sin, but the gospel always brings man back to face and own up to his responsibility for his evil actions. Jesus' statements stimulated healthy questions about their souls and obedience to the Lord. Was this impossible work of God apparent in their own lives? Had they given up enough? Did they have eternal life or an eternal lie?

I must be responsible when I think of myself as Christ's agent in this modern world. If not, there are eternal consequences for my soul. Am I wealthy? Have I sufficiently separated my dependence upon wealth to know whether I have really divorced myself from Wealth or am secretly attached and giving private worship to it?[9]

My wife and I have gone through several life-testing seasons that I trust have ensured the genuineness of our non-attachment to Wealth.

While in college, we lost my wife's income, and I had to work part-time and study full-time. We were committed to not going into debt except for a small college loan and mobile home. We were pretty poor and getting ready for overseas missionary life. We couldn't even repair the air

---

[9] I am not speaking negatively of wealth when used in good ways. We have seen wonderfully committed Christians rightly handle their wealth. My main point is to challenge us to think about the decisions we will make so that we can be numbered with those who handled their wealth well. Start with a study on the risks that Nicodemus, one of the wealthiest men in Jerusalem, took.

conditioner in our hot Florida home until we sold the mobile home! But we trusted God. He miraculously supplied our needs in several ways. When I graduated, we sold the mobile home, paid off our school bills, and went to serve the Lord.

I fear our society is too wealthy; credit is too easy to come by. Many Christians avoid the invaluable wisdom that seasons of lack provide. How do we know if we depend on wealth or God? How can churches help Christians discover the inward and deceptive foes of this modern world?

As long as one has wealth, they do not need to trust in God (Rev 3:17). Without the radical shaping of their souls, people will not be able to see that the diabolical trust in riches is not clever but outright dangerous. We are told that:

- Investments are supposed to be good.
- Insurance is a necessity.
- Fat bank accounts show God's glorious provisions.

But can poverty help a man see the motives of his soul? I believe so, but the opportunity for this is rare. It's no wonder the third-world church is much more alive than the church in wealthier economies. Poverty forces a person to realize that he does not need riches to live a full life. He can depend on His heavenly Father to care for His needs.

"With men it is impossible, but not with God; for all things are possible with God."

Jesus' statements here shook the disciples' thinking. They should shake our thinking too. Jesus taught that the evil of a man's heart runs so deep that no matter what he does, he desperately needs a great and divine work in his heart. This fact sets Christianity apart from other religions: there's no room for self-piety (I am holy enough), self-effort (I have done enough to satisfy God), or self-knowledge (I know the right things).

Worth It All!

Mark 10:28-31

Peter began to say to Him, "Behold, we have left everything and followed You." Jesus said, "Truly I say to you, there is no one who has left house or brothers or sisters or mother or father or children or farms, for My sake and for the gospel's sake, but that he shall receive a hundred times as much now in the present age, houses and brothers and sisters and mothers and children and farms, along with persecutions; and in the age to come, eternal life." (Mark 10:28-30)

Life can be confusing. We need clarification. Jesus, in His teaching in Mark 10:21-27, brought the disciples beyond their comfort zone of knowledge. I suspect that you have been in such situations before, where you were so sure of yourself that you felt like you could be the teacher. Yet, upon hearing something disorienting, you were humbled, maybe broken.

The disciples were sure at one point that Jesus would care for them well. Each of them decided to follow Jesus, after all. Indeed, Jesus could have been more precise about the requirements of following Him, but there's no indication that they ever asked. They were just compelled to be with Jesus. No doubt this is how it was with many of us before we became Christians.

Many of us have entered situations and contracts where we should have been more careful to determine the practical points of the commitment. For example, a school's catalog or a ministry brochure is not where one discovers the sponsoring organization's fundamental ethos. One has to explore the handbook, where one can find all the rules and regulations—the details. Upon reading the handbook, one learns how seriously the organization takes some matters. But similar to Jesus' calling of the disciples, that handbook remains hidden until after one has made some measure of commitment.

After following Jesus for over a year, the disciples had gleaned an understanding of what things would be like. The orientation class was over. Perhaps you remember the feeling of coming back to school after your freshman year: you see the new students with puzzled expressions and full of questions. Maybe you felt smug as you passed off the role of desperately needing answers to the uninitiated. The disciples seemed unaware of their zone of familiarity until Jesus shook them with a few amazing statements.

Effective teachers must go beyond the level of their students' comfort and produce in them an uneasiness with what they know so that they will be more willing to acquire more. Jesus, no doubt, had done this. The way Jesus spoke to the rich man shook them up—the sincere rich man wasn't going to make it into the kingdom of God without giving away all His riches. They suddenly weren't so sure about themselves. We see evidence of this train of thought in Peter's response.

Peter was the disciple who spoke his thoughts out loud. He said, "Behold, we have left everything and followed You." They undoubtedly wondered why someone so contrite, religious, sound, and wealthy had to give away all his wealth. What did they have to give away to gain eternal life? You can sense their desperation to see how they measure up, hoping not to fail the test.

Jesus, in a sense, changed the subject with His answer. At least, the tone of His voice seemed to soften with concern. He sensed that He needed to return to their level and connect their real needs with His "new" teaching. Jesus recognized that His disciples would often be required to make a sacrifice of one kind or another. He appreciated their innocent affection for Him, not wanting any truth to get in the way of the growing relationships between Himself and each disciple. Jesus illustrated a powerful equation.[10]

The disciples felt very vulnerable at this point, but Jesus wisely comforted and encouraged them in the decisions they made and would continue to need to make.[11]

Quite some time ago, I sensed God wanted to bring a change over my life and those of my family. God was using a

---

[10] Cross-cultural missionaries have left the most but have also testified of how they have gained the most. One good brother, Wes Milne, had just retired after 62 years of serving in both China and Taiwan. He mostly cared for delinquent boys. This lifetime bachelor has more sons than all of us! Wherever he went in the world, he had an "adopted" son who lovingly cared for him.

[11] Many decisions appear to be one-time decisions, but the reality is that life decisions are made up of many smaller decisions. The difference is that, with the smaller decisions, our commitments have not changed, so we do not feel the tension.

well-known book, *Experiencing God* (by Blackaby and King), to bring me deeper into my encounters with Him. The truths that He shared with me through this book shook up my then-comfortable world.

I sensed that God wanted to bring me closer to Him. He indicated that two things would need to change in my life to bring me closer as He desired. I knew I needed to get ready for them.[12]

The first area He wanted to change was one of ministry. Could I give up my ministry? I loved my teaching ministry as a pastor. Because I was a full-time pastor, it meant a considerable change in my vocation. The second change was being willing to trust Him for finances. George Mueller trusted God, but would I allow finances to steer God's path for my life or could I allow God to lead and care for me no matter where that leading was? How would the Lord care for my large family of nine (at the time)? I told the Lord I was willing; I wanted to abide in Christ.

Looking back, I can now see that God asked me to give up what I prized to receive more. The pathway was not always easy, however. My wife and I were astounded that God would ask for such significant sacrifices, but we also sensed that they were just the beginning of many more shifts in how we lived our lives. Ultimately, we put the need for security and knowledge of the future in God's hands so that He could work out whatever good He wanted in our lives.

---

[12] God used this and other circumstances to start my ministry, Biblical Foundations for Freedom (BFF).

The world has often significantly shaped our expectations so that we are not willing to fully commit to Christ and His call to share the gospel. We are reluctant and sometimes unwilling to step into a life of unknowns. As a society, we can plan our own lives. We are the ones who make our futures. God, however, assures His disciples, including us, that He will specifically watch over our needs as we faithfully step into the unknown.

Capsizing Religion

Mark 3:1-6

And He entered again into a synagogue; and a man was there with a withered hand. And they were watching Him to see if He would heal him on the Sabbath, in order that they might accuse Him. And He said to the man with the withered hand, "Rise and come forward!" And He said to them, "Is it lawful on the Sabbath to do good or to do harm, to save a life or to kill?" But they kept silent. And after looking around at them with anger, grieved at their hardness of heart, He said to the man, "Stretch out your hand." And he stretched it out, and his hand was restored. And the Pharisees went out and immediately began taking counsel with the Herodians against Him, as to how they might destroy Him. (Mark 3:1-6)

Have you ever been scared by the advice, "Just go to church?" Have you ever considered what the average person experiences when they go to the average church (whatever average might mean)?

Jesus discovered early on that "going to church" could be very uncomfortable. He got upset about how religion got in the way of God's business. Church in His day had become just another place where politicking took place. The venue was different, but the same struggle for personal acceptance happened within the temple walls as in the assembly places of Rome.

Fortunately, at this point, Jesus was not kicked out. Those who had devised evil got up and left in a huff.

What is your experience at church? Could the structure and our expectations of each service have stripped the Lord's ministry from where we would most expect to find it? This account shows how the 'church' attempted to shut out Jesus' ministry of God's love.

Jesus regularly attended synagogue, just as we would attend church. Interestingly, we can call a church 'synagogue' because it means the same thing and functions the same way. They both mean 'an assembly' or 'gathering.' God's people worshipped, learned, and ministered at the synagogue. Leaders would be chosen and made responsible for caring for the people.

Church leaders are responsible for overseeing the ministry, like helping people meet God, teaching, find healing, and help. The problem, in this case, originated not with Sabbath rules or healing but with the teachers who were so intent on preserving "their ministry" and their respectable positions that they were not at all open to how God might want to accomplish perfectly good things in their midst. Maybe we should ask, "How many church leaders would welcome an itinerant young preacher to come in and heal one of their member's withered hands?"

Many churches wouldn't want Him there! They don't believe in healing, and to witness such healing would upset their comfortable zone. They don't want some unordained youngster causing problems during their well-ordered services. Their ministries must be appropriately conducted, not upset by healings and meeting personal needs.

Others argued that Jesus broke the Sabbath. Jesus' disciples, including me, would assert that Jesus properly kept the Sabbath. When a careful look is taken at both their attitudes and the actual teaching of the Sabbath, however, we find that external use of these teachings can be used to keep God out of church more than in the church.

After Jesus called the man with the withered hand forward to stand in front of everyone, He asked an important question, "Is it lawful on the Sabbath to do good or harm, to save a life or to kill?" Jesus' question had a dual purpose: it taught the meaning of the Sabbath and exposed the teachers' evil intentions.

The essence of the Sabbath is to preserve and keep the well-being of man. God doesn't need a sabbath; man does. God built it into our biology and the foundation of the universe; taking a sabbath is one method of caring for ourselves so that we can be well and live good lives in response to His provision. The Sabbath keeps man from oppression and slavery and redeems him into God's presence and purpose. Being forbidden to work frees people to think of themselves apart from their jobs. They are more than laborers; they are also worshippers. We should all be filled with acts of goodness on the Sabbath! What a different place the world would be if we retired from our profit and ego-making schemes and instead focused on caring for people as God directs us in acts of mercy and service.

Jesus exposed these leaders as being the ones who broke the Sabbath. They erred in three significant ways:

- They had no compassion for the man with a withered hand.
- They sought the opportunity to accuse rather than help Jesus.
- They plotted with the Herodians on the Sabbath to destroy Jesus. (They "immediately" did it.)

One would think that they would have spotted their inconsistency, but they were so caught up in assailing Jesus that they were not attuned to what God, the Maker of the Sabbath, desired. Jesus dared to interfere with the accepted religious assumptions so that God's love could more effectively reach people's lives. If a ministry isn't meeting the needs of broken and hurting people, it is not worth keeping.

These revelations have challenged me to be more aware of what God wants to accomplish in our churches. I am often intimidated and even ruled by protocol, even though what we do today might be different than what they did in the New Testament church in Jesus' day. May God deliver me from being so sensitive to what people consider acceptable. We want God to reach in and meet the real needs of His people. How we structure church services and our expectations in those services often makes it difficult to help people as Jesus did.

Mark 3:7-8 describes how people flocked to hear Jesus outside the synagogue by the sea. We would do much better to care for people rather than stay caught up with conducting well-structured services. Maybe more people would come to church—to Jesus—if they had some hope of being ministered to while worshiping Him.

The Family of Jesus

Mark 3:31-35

And His mother and His brothers arrived, and standing outside they sent word to Him, and called Him. And a multitude was sitting around Him, and they said to Him, "Behold, Your mother and Your brothers are outside looking for You." And answering them, He said, "Who are My mother and My brothers?" And looking about on those who were sitting around Him, He said, "Behold, My mother and My brothers! "For whoever does the will of God, he is My brother and sister and mother." (Mark 3:31-35)

Jesus' teaching often shocks readers and onlookers because of how He treated His family and what He taught. We all have beliefs hidden below our awareness, so we should diligently cultivate awareness of our beliefs. We live according to these beliefs, whether they are biblical or not. The crowd here made the average accommodation for His family's arrival and began to draw Jesus' attention to them. There was a social protocol. If you or I were part of this crowd, we, too, would have given particular preference to the Rabbi's family.

Jesus was expected to pay special attention to the arrival of His family members. A formal situation, such as a public address at an amphitheater, would have been handled differently, but this was a more casual gathering. Yet, the crowd still saw the importance of Jesus greeting His family.

Jesus did not carry a cell phone. His family had no easy or straightforward way to get in touch with Him. The crowd operated on the undergirding belief that family members have priority over relationships with others. The people in the crowd understood this and let Jesus know His family was there.

What were Jesus' options? He could have taken a break and gone to see them. Or, if He was in the middle of a message, He certainly could have passed a message on, telling them that He would be with them shortly. They would have understood.

Jesus' answer, however, did not seem to acknowledge this priority, at least at first glance. Jesus' answer surprised His followers and His family; it surprised us, the readers. Yet, the more we think through His answer, the more we should realize that He did understand and accept the importance of caring for family members. The only difference was that the family members He included numbered far more than those who made up His immediate family.

How big was Jesus' family? In Mark 1:1, we read that Jesus was the Son of God. He came to earth to accomplish a mission. In a sense, we understand that all mankind is related to Him because the lineage of all mankind can be traced to Adam, "the son of God" (cf. Luke 3:38). We are all related to each other in some way. By stating what He did,

Jesus was not diminishing the value of His immediate family, but He was helping the crowd understand how big His family was. To Jesus, the crowd was not made up of mere strangers. Each of them stood in the critical line of mankind, which He now shared. However, let us not miss one critical component of Jesus' inclusion.

Jesus said, "For whoever does the will of God, he is My brother and sister and mother." He stopped short of saying His family included everyone. We cannot say He would equally identify with everyone on earth. Adam could, but Jesus, the second Adam, was forming a new family. Only those born from above can enter the kingdom (or family) of God. Jesus chose the words "whoever does the will of God" to characterize His family members. These words can be easily applied to our lives.

Exclusivity

Those who do not carry out God's will are not part of Jesus' family. If we do not belong to Jesus' family, we miss out on the most remarkable thing. We might be near enough to Him to hear Him speak, but unless we are part of His family, we will be considered strangers in eternity. We will hear the laughter, the warmth, the love—but we will not be part of it.

Characteristics

Jesus described His family members: each member "does the will of God." One could say that obedience to God is in their blood. They love to do what God desires. But according to Jesus, those who call God "Father" but refuse to do His will betray their true heritage. They do not belong to Jesus' family, the family of God, but to another.

God's timing for this message struck hard at my heart. He was testing me for compromise. Such tests came fast and furious. They force me to answer the question, "Do I do God's will?" I say I am His, but do I do His will?

A few examples come to mind. First, there was a time I planned poorly and didn't allow sufficient time for worship on the Lord's Day. Yes, I listened to sermons on our long ride home, but I could have more carefully worked out my schedule so that my whole family would have worshiped with me on the Lord's Day.

Another time, I couldn't resolve the tension over a class another person had scheduled for my wife and me on the Lord's Day. I say I want to do God's will but then let myself do those things that I have no peace about doing on Sunday. The culture wants to squeeze me into compromise. Where does one stop? How does one stop?

My soul was in great turmoil and anguish over this situation. I couldn't see a way to resolve it.

- On the one hand, my wife was seven months pregnant. She did not want to change her care provider for the delivery. I knew how important seeing a regular midwife was to her, yet we didn't have insurance or money for a "normal" hospital delivery (with the midwife).

- On the other hand, I loved God. I knew He didn't want a required midwife class to distract me from His day (Sunday was the only day the class was available at the time). The Lord asked me not to compromise, testing me to see if I would do God's will.

God strengthened my faith and clarity of His will. Even in my devotional time, He spoke through David in 1 Samuel, where, in chapter 20, God miraculously protected David. Yet in the following chapter, David compromised despite God's miraculous protection. Under pressure, he lied and acted like a madman. He relied on his resources, and as a consequence of depending on himself, his lies destroyed a village of priests (chapter 22). I didn't want to compromise. But what could I do?

Despite intense inner pressure, I called the particular medical class' teacher and brought up my concerns about having the class on the Lord's Day. Without this class, we would not be able to have this baby at home. We would have no place for the baby to be born! We had no money for backup plans.

The next day, I got a call back from the nurse. She said she would teach us at home for a bit more money. I am so glad that God resolved what I truly felt was irresolvable.

I cried out to God to help me obey Him and care for my wife. God resolved the irresolvable to His glory, which left me to delight in being part of Jesus' family. He truly does care for those He calls His own.

Growing Confidence in Jesus

Mark 7:31-37

And again He went out from the region of Tyre, and came through Sidon to the Sea of Galilee, within the region of Decapolis. And they brought to Him one who was deaf and spoke with difficulty, and they entreated Him to lay His hand upon him. And He took him aside from the multitude by himself, and put His fingers into his ears, and after spitting, He touched his tongue with the saliva; and looking up to heaven with a deep sigh, He said to him, "Ephphatha!" that is, "Be opened!" And his ears were opened, and the impediment of his tongue was removed, and he began speaking plainly. And He gave them orders not to tell anyone; but the more He ordered them, the more widely they continued to proclaim it. And they were utterly astonished, saying, "He has done all things well; He makes even the deaf to hear, and the dumb to speak." (Mark 7:31-37)

Astonished. Utterly astonished. Their positive impression of Jesus was growing in leaps and bounds. Every encounter with Jesus was like entering and exploring a new, exciting room in a rich, lavish mansion. The disciples were party to everything going on—they were not just learning catechism, principles, or techniques. They were learning to trust Jesus with every one of their problems.

An encounter with Jesus was a life-changing experience. This was true for His immediate disciples and the members of the crowd. No matter how often Jesus told the crowd to be quiet about what He had done, they were compelled to tell others about their experiences.

Jesus' instructions were incompatible with the joy in their souls. He was being practical and humble. But they couldn't stay quiet in their astonishment, liberation, and exhilaration. Let's take a closer look at what happened.

Wherever Jesus went and no matter the situations He encountered, He radically changed things for the better. Jesus had just traveled over sixty miles from another city (in the region of Tyre). He had gone away to get a break and spend quality time with His disciples. But His ministry followed Him there too. Those who sought Him out were sad, broken, and despondent. Many of them had to be brought by another person, perhaps because they didn't know that Jesus could help them or because they couldn't come on their own. The latter was the case with the man in this story. "They brought to Him one who was deaf and spoke with great difficulty." There couldn't have been a more complex case! After all, this person's problems were apparent to all.

I wonder if the crowd saw this man lying by the roadside and figured Jesus could help him, or maybe they were testing

Mark 7:31-37 Growing Confidence in Jesus

Jesus to see what He could do. They—probably referring to the crowd, though the scriptures aren't specific—brought him to Jesus. Jesus knew several things about this man:

- His case was challenging. We can see Jesus' elaborate healing measures.

- Jesus resisted "impressing" the crowd by healing the man in private.

- Jesus cared about the man's state and did not care about His own reputation. He told the crowd not to say anything about this miracle.

Jesus did not heal the man as the crowd probably expected. He shattered the simple "lay hands on" means of healing this time. Instead, Jesus stuck His fingers in the man's ears and touched his tongue with His spit. Lastly, He called to God and commanded, "Be opened." Parts of this process might seem repulsive, but the healing was immediate.

A GROWING FAITH

| I see Jesus at work. | My faith is increasing. | I belief Jesus can help others. | I bring hurting people to Jesus. | I tell others about Jesus. |

Another broken man was made whole. The crowd said, "He has done all things well; He makes even the deaf to hear and the dumb to speak." Confidence in Jesus' power began to grow. With the conclusion of this miracle, it's easy to imagine how the crowd might have begun thinking about whom they might bring to Jesus for healing.

When I engage in this story, I can't help but think about my beliefs about Jesus. The best test is to consider whom I have brought to Jesus lately. Of course, we know that Jesus is not physically present, but is He not yet still alive today? Do we not acknowledge that Jesus can now do anything He did then? Do we, as Christ's disciples, not acknowledge that He still desires to do those helpful things?

The problem is that we, myself included, need more faith. You may still be in the process of determining whether Jesus can or wants to do miracles today. We have such little faith.

Our meager faith is the reason we rarely see great things happen. When we do not see great things happen, our impression of Jesus becomes rather stuffy and rigid; we think of Him only as a good teacher. But certainly, this is not the impression the disciples, the crowd, or the healed man had! What kind of impression should I have of Jesus? Jesus is the Son of God. He is to be believed and followed. What Jesus am I following? Is it the real One or an imposter that I can easily fit into my life?

Each meeting with Jesus should be an eye-opening encounter. Each time the body of Christ, the church, stands in His presence, we should be humbled and amazed at His glory. Isn't this the purpose of coming before Him? Our Lord wants us to have faith-empowered lives.

The small amount of faith I have humbles me and compels me to pray. Feel free to join me.

"Dear Lord, your person and work are amazing. Why are my eyes so blind to your great person? Speak "Be opened!" to my eyes of faith so that I might see You for who You are. Forgive me. I am so rarely excited that I don't tell many people about You. If I do venture to say anything, I solely focus on how nice the church is. God, please change this, starting now. Let me start to see Jesus as He is. Fortify my faith so that I can bring anyone to You for help and healing. In Jesus' name, Amen."

A Word on Christian Suffering

John 15:1-2

I am the true vine, and My Father is the vinedresser. Every branch in Me that does not bear fruit, He takes away; and every branch that bears fruit, He prunes it, that it may bear more fruit. (John 15:1-2)

Pain and suffering. No one likes suffering, but most of us will endure some form of it during our lives. Sometimes the pain is prolonged and dull, whereas, at other times, it is brief yet stabbing. Suffering is a topic that is hard to understand in our culture, perhaps because it does not vibe with modern man's quest for pleasure.

No one wants to suffer, yet people must endure pain. There are no easy answers for those who go through agonizing times. Yet this is why I am fascinated with Jesus' words about pruning. Most of us are shy to speak or even think that God is involved with a person's grief and agony. One reason for this may be that many believe pain is incompatible with God's love. Others, not understanding God's good purpose in suffering, get bitter. Jesus' approach to the problem of suffering is refreshingly different!

Jesus faced people's pain every day and saw the suffering of many. People would bring the sickest and most troubled individuals to His feet, and He would bring His Masterful touch of healing. Jesus understands suffering more than we could ever know; He also knows that when we endure suffering as His people, God our Father has a loving purpose.

Jesus is the vine. The vinedresser is God, who cares for the whole vine. While verse 1 is clear, verse 2 needs to be clarified. Here, Jesus speaks about two kinds of branches, both of which have something done to them. However, verse 2 has a translation problem many are unaware of, which impedes a clear understanding of God's teaching. To clarify, Jesus is speaking about two kinds of branches.

Every branch	in Me	1) does not bear fruit	He takes away (lit. lifts up)	
		2) that bears fruit	He prunes it	that it may bear more fruit

There are two things in common with these branches. First, they both are branches. Second, they are both "in Me."[13] Because of the poor translation, many skip right over the phrase "in Me" and only apply it to the second kind of branch. Each kind of branch will suffer some "testings," but the commonality stops there.

---

[13] Although it does not use "in Me" two times, the structure of the sentence implies this. If the second verse did not imply "in Me," then He would have made a contrast with the first such as "not in Me."

The First Type of Branch

The first type of branch describes those branches that do not bear fruit. Many suggest that this barrenness proves that they are the same as those branches in verse 6, "If anyone does not abide in Me, he is thrown away as a branch, and dries up; and they gather them, and cast them into the fire, and they are burned." But this is not an accurate interpretation.

What happens to each of these branches is very different: the latter is burnt up, but the first is "lifted up." How unfortunate it is that several versions translate this word as "takes away," further complicating a proper understanding of the passage. Even the NIV uses the inappropriate translation of "cut off." The translators clearly do not understand grape plants; if they did, they would use the obvious and standard definition "to lift up."

These unproductive branches deserve to be cut off, but they are not treated this way. Instead, they are lifted up, which refers to the way a vinedresser would raise the branches fallen upon the ground, clean them, and then tie them up with other healthier branches.[14] When lying in the mud, they receive no sunlight and have no hope for producing fruit. This is an excellent description of wayward and stubborn Christians who need to be cleaned. The Caretaker focuses not on fruit at this point but on survival. There is no

---

[14] I am thankful to Bruce Wilkinson who mentions this in his excellent book, "Secrets of the Vine." He gleaned the truth from a vine keeper.

doubt that the cleansing process gets rather rough at times, including discipline and chastisement (cf. Hebrews 12).

The Second Type of Branch

The second branch does bear fruit. Of course, it also abides in the vine; otherwise, it wouldn't bear fruit. The fruit represents different but wholesome effects originating from God—from His truth and love. The sap from the vine (Jesus) flows into His believers' lives, causing fruit to grow.

Jesus, however, also speaks about the process of pruning these fruitful vines. He says that suffering will be part of every believer's life, though it differs. Every good branch will suffer pruning. This pruning is not a careless cutting of the branches to make them shorter—though this is how many of us feel about pain. When we get struck hard, we tend to conclude that God doesn't care about us, but the opposite is true!

I had a few apple trees for a few years and decided it was time for a good pruning. When I finished, I was proud of my "pruning" job. "They should bear great fruit next year," I thought. I was so careful to get every small branch so that the trees could focus their energy on producing fruit through the big branches and bear forth lots of big luscious fruit.

Something wasn't right, however. The blossoms the following spring were very sparse. I came up with many reasons for this: the winter was extremely harsh, or there must be something wrong with the trees. I think I called the company that sold them to me to see if they could explain why there were no blossoms. I discovered the problem later.

When pruning, I had cut off all the tiny little branches where the blossoms and fruit grow! I was unaware of how to prune correctly for a productive harvest. Our Heavenly Father, fortunately, is totally unlike me. He knows precisely what He is doing. Although I intended to help my trees bear fruit, I was ignorantly reckless. About two years later, a neighbor came by and showed me that I was pruning them all wrong. I finally did get a good crop, thanks to him.

To speak of pain and suffering is not easy. It is risky business for people to ask the tough question, "Why does God allow suffering?" This question gets worse when it is phrased, "Why does God allow [fill in the blank] to happen?"

In this passage, Jesus partly resolves the problem of suffering by saying, "He prunes it, that it may bear more fruit." Jesus doesn't deny God's involvement in a believer's suffering. Sometimes when we hear about things happening to Christians in faraway places, we are left with the impression that God allows suffering among His sheep and doesn't care. Jesus challenges this and says, "He prunes it, that it may bear more fruit."

Jesus is intent on bringing God into our perspective of suffering. God Himself orchestrates the problematic situation as the vinedresser. Yes, God does allow evil forces to oppress His people, and yes, He does tolerate the rise of wicked men for a while.

But He promises, as our vinedresser, to supervise the process with a greater goal in mind. None of this is done in vain. It will hurt, but the pain will be carefully monitored and purposeful. We must trust His trained, sovereign hands in this process. God has not left us alone. Quite the contrary, He closely works with us so that we may have more fruitful lives.

Jesus did not say that we are the reason things go wrong to deserve such pruning. In fact, it's often when we do things well, when we are most fruitful, that we become ready for pruning. It's a horticultural fact that bigger and more plentiful fruit grows when branches are pruned back. The implication here is clear: God wants His life to flow through us at a larger volume and faster rate so that more of Him can shine through us and out into the world. He wants us to bear more fruit and reap greater incredible eternal blessings.

Pruning times are challenging. When I started the ministry in 2000, the Lord took away many vital aspects of life—a typical job, close friends and their support, good fellowship with Christians, a sense of belonging, financial stability, etc. Not everything was taken away, but many cherished things were. This reminds me so much of what a brother shared recently from Deuteronomy 8.5, "Thus you are to know in your heart that the LORD your God was disciplining you just as a man disciplines his son."

God's pruning action shows that He is actively working in our lives. We must take this truth and store it deep in our hearts. When suffering occurs, we must refuse to think God has abandoned us. Pruning is part of His long-term care plan for our lives. If we forget how the Vinedresser best cares for us, we may become confused and doubtful, so we must cultivate a deep trust in and love for this process so that we, in time, can bear much more glorious fruit.

The processes of lifting up and pruning both hurt; each requires pain. "Lifting up" refers to discipline and the elimination of sin, whereas pruning pushes us toward the process of self-denial. There is no better place to see this than the self-denial in effect when Jesus, our Master, died on the cross for His people's sins.

Maybe Jesus pointed to the pruned branch of a grapevine that bore many grapes, their strong scent filling the air as He taught about the vines. He might have swallowed hard as He said these words, knowing He was on the way to the Mount of Olives to be betrayed. He knew He would be pruned so that He might bear even more fruit (Is 53:11-12). Although evil men might have treated Jesus cruelly and unjustly, it was all carefully governed by the Great Vinedresser.

To be more like Jesus, we must stay focused through these times of pruning, trusting God's good purpose through it all.

Genuine Worship

Mark 12:28-34

And one of the scribes came and heard them arguing, and recognizing that He had answered them well, asked Him, "What commandment is the foremost of all?" Jesus answered, "The foremost is, 'Hear, O Israel! The LORD our God is one LORD; and you shall love the LORD your God with all your heart, and with all your soul, and with all your mind, and with all your strength.'"

"The second is this, 'You shall love your neighbor as yourself.' There is no other commandment greater than these." And the scribe said to Him, "Right, Teacher, You have truly stated that He is one; and there is no one else besides Him; and to love Him with all the heart and with all the understanding and with all the strength, and to love one's neighbor as himself, is much more than all burnt offerings and sacrifices." And when Jesus saw that he had answered intelligently, He said to him, "You are not far from the kingdom of God." And after that, no one would venture to ask Him any more questions. (Mark 12:28-34)

Jesus' disciples walked beside Him for three years. One great benefit was that they heard the messages that Jesus the Messiah (lit., Christ) shared with everyone.

Jesus was not just a highly popular park preacher. He spoke on serious topics and could answer the scholarly religious leaders of His day. Jesus' answers somehow cut right to the heart of all the teachers' long dialogues. Christ knew and shared the answers to common life questions. Though the Jewish teachers asked questions intending to confound and confuse Jesus, each of His answers further affirmed that He came from the Father.

One question a scribe asked seemed innocent enough that any child might ask it: "What is the greatest commandment of all?"

This question was different because the person asking it didn't seem to be asking out of trickery but from sincerity. Being a scribe, he knew much about God's Word, but perhaps he got caught up in fulfilling the commands and lost track of whom he was obeying! He should have loved God above all. Jesus' answer to this simple question amazed the crowd because it was, in turn, simple, truthful, and powerful.

The answer astounded this earnest seeker. As a scribe, he busied himself with writing copies of the precious scriptures. Jesus' answer was simply a quote from the Old Testament (Deut 6:4). The command, however, to wholly love God was all-demanding, a command that would take every bit of attention the man had to spare.

With one quick line, the Almighty One revealed the emptiness of the Judaistic religion. Attention to the commands without love for God was inadequate. Only one thing matters: do I love God wholly? Anything not built upon this command is best considered unimportant.

Religious habits can impress others, but they are vain without God. Such religious habits, of course, include those of Christianity too.

I have studied the Bible for many years, and over time, I've gone through seasons where I viewed my time reading the Bible as routine and mundane rather than an opportunity to express affection and deepen my desire to know God. I had lost the deep yearning I once had to know Him and His Word more so that I could better obey Him.

There have been times when I was eager to finish my reading so that I could deal with other pressing activities. At these times, my mind was easily distracted and worried as I read. I don't think I'd generally dare to say that reading God's Word or studying theology in these states is fruitless, but it had become so at different points in my case.

This scribe was spiritually alert and responded to Jesus by saying that loving God was "much more than all burnt offerings and sacrifices." This expression might be hard for us to identify with, but consider it this way: "We are to love God more than attending any church service or serving in ministry." The scribe was not saying that burnt offerings and sacrifices (or in our case, church services and ministry) were unimportant. However, the love we have for God should outshine these other activities.

When at church, I sometimes ask myself, "What is on my heart? Am I meditating on the greatness and glory of God, or am I more interested in talking to someone after church? Do I love God?" That last one is the big question.

I also consider what I talk about on the way home. Do I think about sports, clothes, or something else? Is my mind on Him, or am I simply critiquing the worship service? When our hearts are excited, they should foster a positive response to the worship of God by saying, "God is so good. What did I discover about God today?" What good is attending church if we don't express our love for God? It would be like dating someone you decisively know you don't want to marry!

Jesus fittingly described the scribe as not being far from the kingdom. Is it possible to step away from the pride of our religious duties and allow ourselves to be captivated by the love of the awesome and living God?

Being close to His kingdom is not good enough. We must go in—and not just part of us, either. We must enter His holy presence with all of our "heart, and with all your soul, and with all your mind, and with all your strength," or not at all. May God's Spirit powerfully work in us all.

Dreams to Dust

Mark 13:1-3

And as He was going out of the temple, one of His disciples said to Him, "Teacher, behold what wonderful stones and what wonderful buildings!" And Jesus said to him, "Do you see these great buildings? Not one stone shall be left upon another which will not be torn down." And as He was sitting on the Mount of Olives opposite the temple, Peter and James and John and Andrew were questioning Him privately. (Mark 13:1-3)

You can't blame them. They were excited and couldn't keep that excitement under wraps! They expressed their amazement and delight in the beauty of the buildings, the splendor glowing before their eyes.

For the Jews in Jesus' day, the glistening golden temple on the Mount of Olives was truly an impressive sight, even for the disciples. Judaism exhibited their temple proudly, with gilded gold. The Roman fort lodged on one corner of the temple mount should have stripped away any romantic notions that all was well, yet even still, the glory of these buildings radiated the Jewish heart. After all, they stood for everything that made them Jewish, or so they thought.

Jesus understood people. He knew the buildings impressed His disciples. Their words, "Teacher, behold what wonderful stones and what wonderful buildings," allowed Jesus to see into their minds and hearts. He noted two things: what they were excited about and not excited about.

Excitement enables people to overlook problems and difficulties. How many engaged couples ignore complex problems due to the anticipation of getting married to the one they love? Jesus felt compelled to give them a reality check.

Those significant buildings were soon coming down! "Do you see these great buildings? Not one stone shall be left upon another which will not be torn down." Jesus was referencing the Second Temple, which they frequented. (Herod the Great greatly expanded it to please the Jews.)

Do we chase after the things that gleam? Do not our hearts follow the golden reflections? The terrorists did a critical study of America before they chose their 9/11 targets.[15] What buildings were more internationally well-known than the 110-story World Trade Center? Standing more than a quarter of a mile high near the heart of the stock exchange, this monument spoke of world power and influence. The Pentagon stood for the world's mightiest army. Would we understand if Jesus told us that the World Trade buildings would not soon be there? Could we believe it? How could they not be there?

Unsurprisingly, disbelief was the disciples' exact response. Incredulous. Those massive stones couldn't be moved. In 70

---

[15] 911, this number, stands for September 11.

A.D., though, just as Jesus said, those temple stone walls came down. The invading Roman army made sure of this because they wanted the gold laid between each of the temple stones. In a similarly tragic scene, the twin World Trade Towers are also no longer present.[16]

The message is the same. When buildings or other worldly things call up our amazement and wonder, we can be sure we have vested our values with them to some degree. They become our idols, symbolizing what we treasure and hope for. One might think this was not bad for the Jews, but the kingdom of God is not capsulized in buildings or their organized religion. Jesus told the Samaritan woman in John 4:21, "Woman, believe Me, an hour is coming when neither in this mountain, nor in Jerusalem, shall you worship the Father."

Those who governed the temple were the very ones who put Jesus Christ to death! There is a world of difference between God's kingdom and the world's kingdom.

God's kingdom in America rests neither with the Trade Towers nor the Pentagon. They are imposters that attract people's attention and fascination. They can all be gone in a matter of minutes or hours. These buildings were indeed significant, but they deceived; they represented a power and influence that cannot and does not last. Every other building on this earth will likewise crumble. These large events serve

---

[16] Understand and deal with world tragedies, click here.
www.foundationsforfreedom.net/Topics/Jd/Tragedy00.html

as examples that lead us to reexamine what we truly treasure.

Jesus' prediction didn't bring this disaster; He only let people know so that their souls would not die with the temple's destruction. We can only rest on the wings of hope when we turn our eyes from man-made monuments and back onto God.

The disaster came because they rejected the Kingdom of God, not because they embraced it. Disaster came to America not because Americans pursued God's kingdom plans but because they sought and applauded their own achievements.

A Faith of Action

Mark 11:27-33

They came again to Jerusalem. And as He was walking in the temple, the chief priests and the scribes and the elders came to Him, and began saying to Him, "By what authority are You doing these things, or who gave You this authority to do these things?" And Jesus said to them, "I will ask you one question, and you answer Me, and then I will tell you by what authority I do these things. Was the baptism of John from heaven, or from men? Answer Me." They began reasoning among themselves, saying, "If we say, 'From heaven,' He will say, 'Then why did you not believe him?' But shall we say, 'From men'?"—they were afraid of the people, for everyone considered John to have been a real prophet. Answering Jesus, they said, "We do not know." And Jesus said to them, "Nor will I tell you by what authority I do these things." (Mark 11:27-33)

Tension always exists between the thinkers and the doers, those who plan and those who act. However, we cannot categorically say that those who take action do not think.

We all are probably more concerned about the presence of extremists since the 9/11 terrorist act. But far from not thinking and planning, they fully calculated their plan, from the costs to the timing. Their thinking led them into wrong and hateful activities that caused many thousands of deaths.

The conflict between those who think and those who act came to a head when they accused Jesus of being too much of a doer in his actions. Some called Him an extremist, a danger to society. Despite what He was called, He was willing for His belief to shape His actions.

I am not positive why Jesus' actions provoked such a formal response from the leaders in the Jewish community—both religious and civil. They interrupted Jesus' public teaching and challenged him regarding the authority He claimed ruled His actions.

Perhaps, they pointed to some tables and chairs Jesus had broken when He drove out the money changers from the temple area as they challenged Him. They might have better tolerated a teacher who only spoke or taught—but Jesus did more than talk; He took action.[17]

Present-day ministerial training focuses too much on acquiring knowledge. There have been some good church movements that have kept the church from going astray. These movements have stirred the church into praying, worshiping, evangelizing, and caring for the poor. But we must admit that the typical seminary is conditioning its leaders to think rather than do. Their pride in knowledge and tradition sometimes supersedes their confidence in the scriptures, a conditioning that gradually pollutes the

---

[17] Mark 11:27-33 can be compared to similar passages: Matthew 21:23-27 and Luke 20:1-8. Each time the charge came in the last week of Jesus' earthly life and one or two days after the cleansing of the temple.

Mark 11:27-33 A Faith of Action

congregations they serve. They are proud of their faith, even though it is dead.

> Even so faith, if it has no works, is dead, being by itself. But someone may well say, "You have faith, and I have works; show me your faith without the works, and I will show you my faith by my works." (James 2:17-18)

Intriguingly, the Jewish leaders, the chief priests, scribes, and elders (what a gang!) challenged Jesus on the things He was doing rather than what He was teaching. Though they could publicly only comment on the action in the temple courts, they had serious problems with what Jesus did outside the temple courts. Jesus' ministry—miracles, healings, etc.—was all closely interwoven with His teaching.

The church can teach what it wants; the world only starts to get concerned when the church starts practicing its faith. The world can tolerate a dead faith that produces no fruit. Why? Because a person's dead faith won't get in the way; it can be quickly shoved aside and compromised. Many Christians have yet to learn how to integrate action with their faith.

As long as we focus on these expressions of faith—abortion clinic protests, marches for Jesus, ministering to the homeless, buying computers for inner-city children, etc.—we will have missed the picture. The issue is not to mimic others but to find what God's Word is saying and respond to it as He leads us.[18]

There are an infinite number of ways to do our Father's will. But we need to get close to God if we want Him to shape our faith into life-changing actions. If we do not get close enough to hear Him, we will not know what He wants us to do. This intimacy with God calls for inner and outer transformation, the former preceding the latter.

The Lord won't ask us to do things when we aren't ready. There's no sense in doing so. It wouldn't make sense for the government to require citizens to file their taxes before receiving their documents, would it? There are enough commands in the Bible that many of His people totally and purposely ignore. Just as Gideon trembled when the Lord commanded him to tear down his father's idols (Judges 6:25), we tremble in our weakness. How difficult it is to do what He wants! I have often boasted, "I will do all you want," but often find myself hard of hearing when He speaks.

I typically fear doing the specific activities the Lord requests. Like Moses with his problem of stumbling speech, I can think of many excuses to rationalize my way out of the command to "go and evangelize that person over there," "write an editorial for the newspaper on a touchy topic," or "give that drunk person a ride home." He gives us

---

[18] Many join prefabricated events rather than do things out of the convictions of their hearts. A following can disappear quickly! We shouldn't be afraid to start somewhere, even if that means participating in other people's convictions, to help discern what the Lord has us to do, but we should be seeking how the Lord wants to use us specifically—be Lord, not people, directed.

opportunities to obey so that our faith can overcome our fears and doubts.

Jesus knew the leaders needed more time to contemplate their question on His authority to cleanse the temple yard of the merchant sellers (Mark 11:15-18), so He asked them a difficult question. He could not have done those things without His Father's instruction. But Jesus wasn't there for publicity. His actions weren't gimmicks to bring attention to Himself. Jesus cared about how people disdained His Father's house of prayer. Jesus switched the question back to them and confused them.

There's a long list of things Jesus did on earth. John states that the list could fill all the books ever written! "And there are also many other things which Jesus did, which if they were written in detail, I suppose that even the world itself would not contain the books which were written" (John 21:25).

The religious leaders did not come to Him with problems about His teaching but because of what He did. If we are true followers of Jesus, we should, like Jesus, also have works that bring the world into a confrontation with the holy Creator. But alas, we are too often content to believe alone without works. We ought to ask ourselves the following question: "Is there sufficient evidence by which others know I am a follower of Jesus Christ?"[19]

---

[19] This question has been around in different forms for many years. I hope it remains! It's worth asking ourselves often.

The Felling of Fame

Mark 2:1-2

> When He had come back to Capernaum several days afterward, it was heard that He was at home. 2 And many were gathered together, so that there was no longer room, not even near the door; and He was speaking the word to them. (Mark 2:1-2)

When I read Mark 2:1-2, I instantly encountered my desire for fame. I stopped reading there, even though the real story of Jesus' healing had yet to be told. The truth I needed to hear had already begun to prick my conscience.

The thoughts of fame came surging in like an exploding bomb filling my mind. I suspect the evil one inserted these thoughts, no doubt trying to lure my heart and make me desire the same kind of recognition as Jesus had.

Once Jesus returned to Capernaum, the crowds gathered around Jesus. There were so many people that no one else could even approach the house where He was. He spoke the Word to them (Mark 2:1-2).

You would think the picture of people running to hear and see Jesus is pleasant. But that wasn't my thought. I found that I was not happy that people were running to Jesus. Rather, my thoughts were more similar to the jealous scribes, gathering evidence against Him. I was thinking neither of Jesus' words to the gathered crowd nor, to my great shame, of the healing and peace He gave the needy. I was so self-absorbed that I couldn't even see Jesus.

I stopped my reading to catch my thoughts. I was sure that I had intended to learn from Jesus when I sat down that day to read God's Word. I read because I delighted in His presence and teaching and wanted Jesus to teach me. As I stopped my reading to capture my thoughts, I wondered if He was exposing something about me. Whether I came up with such thoughts or another entity planted them, I needed to deal with them.

Is it wrong to seek fame? To determine the answer, we must ask ourselves, "Why am I seeking fame?" People usually seek fame because they want to feel important or validated.

The fact of fame is not bad, but the evil of fame thrives in total denial of the facts. True greatness in a Christian context is not measured by how many people gather to listen but by how much you humbly do the will of God. Greatness is to seek and do God's will. As long as we pursue attention to ourselves, our eyes will not be on the Lord. We have nothing but what is given to us. His call and gifts are differently distributed—not based on who we are but on what He wants to accomplish through us (Rom 12:6). The Lord made each one of us; no one is inherently better than anyone else. By His grace, we can get better only because He helps us make better decisions. We do not get better because we are worth more.

Why is it that we have this compulsion to feel important and liked? Thoughts such as, "People like me," "People think I'm smart," or "People think I'm attractive" reveal voids in our hearts. The craving for attention causes us to conclude, though falsely, that attention will fulfill us.

- He focused on doing what His Father said at any cost.
- He loved people and had compassion for them.
- He was willing to turn people and leaders away from following Him.
- He told people not to tell others of His miracles.
- He moved from place to place instead of building a personal kingdom.
- He refused to pile up material things to emphasize His importance.
- He gave up all the attention He had received from others to embrace a cold, cruel cross.
- He was willing to be betrayed by a close companion.

Jesus rightly handled the temptation of fame. Though probably conscious of Himself and what people thought of Him, His awareness didn't drive His actions. He did not act to gain or maintain a crowd; the crowd wasn't necessary. He refused to let their opinions gain prominence in His heart. He focused on what God called Him to accomplish, His

Father's will in His Father's timing and process. He cared more for other people than Himself. Just as Mark 12:30-31 says, He loved His Father, and in loving Him, He loved other people. Jesus came to serve.

Jesus occupied Himself with serving others.

Before a person begins ministry, they must deal with their attitude toward pride. I often wonder how many have been challenged to confront the desire for popularity while training. If the crowd comes first, one will hardly ever be humble enough to deal with this heart issue rightly. I began to resolve this issue in my own heart later in my ministry, but by God's grace, He pointed it out to me.

I took some time to respond to the Spirit's prompting:

- I confessed that I like the attention of others.
- I also confessed that I am often more conscious of myself and people's perception of me than of what God wants of me.
- I repented of this desire for fame and asked the Lord to come like a great storm and break this wall of pride in my life.
- I only want as many people to hear me speak as my Father desires, and with this, I will be pleased even if it means I never speak again.
- I will be content with His choice and will for my life as decreed from eternity. There is nothing more than the grace given to me and to be called His child.

- I furthermore asked the Lord for the determination to seek only my Father's will and the profit of those around me, whether one person or ten thousand.

A Perspective on Worry

Luke 12:25-26

His observations are simple but startling.

And which of you by being anxious can add a single cubit to his life's span? If then you cannot do even a very little thing, why do you worry about other matters? (Luke 12:25-26)

Everyone could answer Jesus' rhetorical question. They knew the answer. We know the answer. Worrying doesn't help our situation! Two questions, like two lenses, are linked here to help us gain a clearer picture of worry.

How often have you caught yourself worrying about a test, a partner, a friend, an appointment, meeting a stranger, being in danger, etc.?

The list of things you might potentially worry about goes on and on. If we made a list of the things we worry about, we would be shocked (or, maybe we wouldn't be). Jesus' observation is accurate: worrying never helps our situation.

Many of us are concerned about our physical features and length of life. These two characteristics both fit the category

—either of height or lifespan.[20] The story is the same. By worrying, we cannot add inches to our height or time to our life. This is indisputable. Jesus says that worrying over these things never does us any good.

I am flexible and tend to worry less often than others. However, I have my own set of failures to tell about. I remember being lined up for my junior high year picture. I was positioned way off to the side, being one of the shortest boys. I despised my shortness, but worry never made me taller. I knew that my friend did not like me more because of my worry.

Jesus' argument is simple: if you or I cannot do a straightforward thing like adding height to our bodies or length to our lives, why should we be anxious about other matters? Jesus uses height as a test case. If we can't affect this, which is evident and measurable, then why should we expect it to help with other matters?

When pastoring in the late nineties, I took a two-week evangelistic trip with a small team to the far eastern edge of Russia. I had just arrived, my first full day and our team went out to eat. I was trying to get my bearings in this new culture and was excited to evangelize on this trip. I could evangelize to the Russians through a translator and directly to the Chinese who came across the border. My bags were

---

[20] A cubit is commonly considered to be 18 inches; some say it also is a measure of time (BAG). The word "picas" (for tiny measurements) comes from this same word (Greek: *pechus*). Life's span, or stature, are equally acceptable translations.

packed heavy, especially with Chinese resources. The Russian literature came in differently. The restaurant we ate at was about a mile from our hotel. As I descended the restaurant steps, I sprained—or broke—my ankle.

I instantly saw my whole trip go up in smoke, but instead of following this line of thought, I decided I would not worry. After all, He had called me here. I babied my foot on the way home; every step caused me to wince in pain. That night, I cried out to God for help. In the morning, my foot was entirely well. I couldn't have made it better. This was something that God needed to care for, and He did. He cared for my ankle and, much more importantly, the souls of men.

When Jesus says that "gaining inches" or "prolonging life" is only a small matter, it's easy to get frustrated—that's easy enough for Him to say! If anyone could add height or time to a life, it would be remarkable. What makes it worse is that He deliberately says "tiniest" or "smallest" thing.[21] I don't think it is a small matter, let alone the smallest of matters. Jesus must be speaking from God's perspective and not ours!

For God, these "stretch" activities are easy. He says, "I stretched out the heavens with My hands" (Isaiah 45:12). For us, however, they are impossible! We cannot govern such circumstances, no matter how much we study, exercise, or dream. Hezekiah cried out to God for a longer life, and He

---

[21] Superlative of short (*elacistov*). This word reminds me of an elastic (rubber) band. To achieve smallest, the elastic needs to be contracted all the way.

granted it to him. But Hezekiah couldn't have done that for himself.

> In those days Hezekiah became mortally ill. And Isaiah the prophet the son of Amoz came to him and said to him, "Thus says the LORD, 'Set your house in order, for you shall die and not live.'" Then he turned his face to the wall, and prayed to the LORD, saying, "Remember now, O LORD, I beseech Thee, how I have walked before Thee in truth and with a whole heart, and have done what is good in Thy sight." And Hezekiah wept bitterly. And it came about before Isaiah had gone out of the middle court, that the word of the LORD came to him, saying, "Return and say to Hezekiah the leader of My people, 'Thus says the LORD, the God of your father David, I have heard your prayer, I have seen your tears; behold, I will heal you. On the third day you shall go up to the house of the LORD. And I will add fifteen years to your life, and I will deliver you and this city from the hand of the king of Assyria; and I will defend this city for My own sake and for My servant David's sake.'" (2 Kings 20:1-6)

Jesus recognizes that such matters are impossible for us but uses these examples to emphasize that all things are equally doable for God. These matters—all those about which we worry—are not things we can control. In the end, only God has control.

Jesus is not saying we should give in to fate and be lazy because things will be as they will be. Not at all! He's trying to emphasize that there are things that are God's affairs. Only He can deal with them, so we ought to let Him deal with them!

Through these two simple questions, Jesus cuts through all the noise—we don't need books about anxiety and worry. We worry because we are trying to take God's affairs into our own hands. We are worried about results, timing, looks, height, acceptance, wealth, etc., but God has made Himself responsible for how tall we are, how long we live, where we are born, how wealthy we are, how we look, and many other matters.

The only solution for our worry is to let God arrange our life plans. I remember praying for parking places, money, people to meet, protection, etc. Jesus constantly lived this way, always seeking the Father's will. I have a long way to go to be consistent, but I am beginning to learn that God has His finger in the details of my life. He rarely announces the details ahead of time, but He does promise to care for me, and that is sufficient.

Worry never helps but only distorts the picture God wants us to see. We need to adopt God's perspective on life to live free from worry.

Overcoming the Fear of Man

Mark 11:27-33

And they came again to Jerusalem. And as He was walking in the temple, the chief priests, and scribes, and elders came to Him, and began saying to Him, "By what authority are You doing these things, or who gave You this authority to do these things?" (Mark 11:27-28)

The fear of man is a common problem, no less for my life than for yours. As I read this passage, my flawed life flashed through my mind. I wondered, "How many times have I failed my Lord and those around me because I gave in to the fear of man?" I knew it was too many times to count.

I was humbled. Convicted. I needed to sit still and pray for a while. In those moments, God started a new work in my life by excavating buried fears. The dead stuff of my life needed to be removed so I could live a full life before God and others.

The fear of man ensnares us, causing us to fail to do what God would have us do. The compromise is made via thoughts, words, or actions in response to our fear, which results in faulty decisions and their consequences.

Jesus' disciples saw their Master face at least four intimidating circumstances in this encounter. They also saw that He did not give in to fear.

• Jerusalem

There is no more significant city where a person would go to gain respect and fame than Jerusalem. If one is received well in the capital, he is received well by the nation. Here was the chance of a lifetime to show Himself as a great Teacher of God.

• The temple of God

Was there a more austere place to display one's knowledge of God than at the temple of God? By being accepted by man and conforming to man's wisdom, He could show Himself to be holy and close to God.

• Confrontation

The confrontation between Jesus and the chief priest, scribes, and elders—a crowd of them—screams compromise. Representatives of the three most respected groups confronted Jesus. At a minimum, there would have been six men, all adorned in ornate, impressive robes, who came to challenge Jesus. Many others undoubtedly accompanied them. (They didn't want to miss this scene!) Jesus was outnumbered. Outflanked. Out-educated. This situation was ripe for compromise for the sake of acceptance.

• Hostility

Their question addressed the core of Jesus' ministry. There were many ways Jesus could have compromised to gain a favorable opinion among the leaders of the people. He could have said, "We are working for the same God. Sorry if there were any misunderstandings." But Jesus did not do this.

The fear of man has, at times, been an actual snare in my life. Jesus, however, was not shaken or scared by the threat of these men's influence. He was not shamed into cowardliness but filled with the Spirit, He responded with wisdom when countering their challenges. I need a fear of God that nullifies intimidation.

Jesus said He would answer their question if they first answered His. Out of politeness, they were required to answer:

> And Jesus said to them, "I will ask you one question, and you answer Me, and then I will tell you by what authority I do these things. Was the baptism of John from heaven, or from men? Answer Me." And they began reasoning among themselves, saying, "If we say, 'From heaven,' He will say, 'Then why did you not believe him?' But shall we say, 'From men'?"—they were afraid of the multitude, for all considered John to have been a prophet indeed. And answering Jesus, they said, "We do not know." And Jesus said to them, "Neither will I tell you by what authority I do these things." (Mark 11:29-33)
>
> "Was the baptism of John from heaven, or from men? Answer me."

Their private discussion is detailed in the last verses. It's easy to imagine the members of these three groups huddled together, trying to come up with the best answer. In the end, they declined to answer. Christ's wisdom can be observed in several ways:

- Jesus did not share God's beautiful truth with skeptics.
- Jesus devised a question that would have them analyze the key issues. In this case, it was authority.
- Jesus confronted them with their guilt. If John the Baptist was from heaven (God), why did they not respect him and take his advice?
- They were afraid of man and refused to answer.

One takeaway I can apply to my life is the need to seek God's wisdom to meet the stubbornness and skepticism of today's secular leaders.

The Spirit of God has spent time excavating my soul. With each situation, He's uncovered another area controlled by my fear of man. It is a humbling experience because it shows me how I've disobeyed God and let down my fellow man. In all reality, the Spirit needed a tractor to do the excavating! I am increasingly amazed at the great grace of God and His patient willingness to work with me.

I need God's grace to hate sin to the same degree He does. Hating sin to such an extent would cause me better to examine my life in light of God's Word. It is now easier to refuse to ignore my guilt or fear of man.

The leaders of the people were unwilling to let God's Word dig deep into their hearts and therefore had no answer for Jesus. They had no Word from God and were caught in the snare of intimidation.

I had many experiences with intimidation when I was a young boy. When people intimidated me, it caused me to become afraid of people. Later, I adopted the belligerent techniques that had worked on me as a boy; raising my voice, using threatening words, grimacing my face, etc., were all long-lasting habits that I needed God's grace to break. None are appropriate, yet all intimidate, which is not God's heart. Should I be surprised when my family members start using these techniques with their siblings? One generation's sins are passed down to another.

May we put to death these intimidating tactics!

Appendix 1: More on Paul J. Bucknell

Paul worked as an overseas church planter during the 1980s and pastored in the United States during the 1990s. God called him to establish Biblical Foundations for Freedom in 2000, and since then, he has actively written, held international Christian leadership training seminars, and served in the local church.

Paul's wide range of materials includes Christian life, discipleship, godly living, leadership training, marriage, parenting, anxiety, Old and New Testament studies, and other spiritual life topics. They can be found in his many books and media-rich training resources.

Paul has been married for more than forty beautiful years. With eight children and eight grandchildren, Paul and his wife Linda continually see God's blessings unfold in their lives.

➡ For more on Paul and Linda and the BFF ministry, check online.]

Appendix 2: Your Personal Notes

Appendix 3: About This Book

Abiding in Christ: Walking with Jesus

Paul J. Bucknell

Abiding in Christ is a step-by-step account of how the Lord drew my heart closer to Him through biblical meditation. After getting me to commit myself further to meditate in His Word, the Lord challenged me to determine whether I believed I could be blessed through those meditation times. This book records some of these "soul encounters" with Jesus through those meditation times.

Old Gospel scenes came alive as I observed what the disciples saw and heard while with Jesus. I asked, "How did Jesus train His disciples in this setting?" I began learning like I never had before. What were once familiar stories now brought tears, a broken heart, and faith-building lessons for the future.

Made in the USA
Monee, IL
13 August 2023